DATE DUE

SEP 20 '80		
OCT 4 '80 OCT 20 '80		
JAN 12 '81		
DEC. 03 '82		
JAN 25 '83		
JAN 29 '85		
GAYLORD		PRINTED IN U.S.A

THE OLD LIGHTHOUSE

*The Story of the
Pacific Garden Mission*

THE OLD LIGHTHOUSE

The Story of the
Pacific Garden Mission

By

JAMES R. ADAIR

MOODY PRESS
CHICAGO

DEDICATION

*To those of God's people
who regularly give and pray
to keep the
Old Lighthouse shining*

"The dayspring from on high hath visited us, to give light to them that sit in darkness and in the shadow of death" (Luke 1:78-79).

TABLE OF CONTENTS

ACKNOWLEDGMENTS

I'M GLAD for the day in 1948 when Ken Anderson, the widely known author of Christian books and producer of gospel films, took a trip to the Orient. It was then that Harry Saulnier, superintendent of Pacific Garden Mission, called to ask me to take over temporarily the editing of the *Pacific Garden Mission News,* a job Ken had been handling. As it turned out, Ken became so involved with books and films on his return to the States that I continued editing the *News.*

It has been a joy working with Harry Saulnier over the years. I have come to love him as a Christian brother and to admire him as a master soul winner. Thus, writing this book about the Mission and the miracles God has wrought at the Old Lighthouse has been a task I have thoroughly enjoyed.

Today, as I was writing this, I received a letter from a man who has strange ideas about the Christian faith. I hope this book will help convince even such skeptics as he that God is still very much in the business of transforming lives broken by sin. The letter writer commented sarcastically, "By and large, the 20th century is a world full of entirely different people, who cannot be helped to live in this world by trying to apply the outmoded, culturally determined, heretical 'old-time religion' you peddle [through Scripture Press and *Power* Magazine]."

If only this man could meet and talk to some of the people whose lives have been transformed at the Mission by the power of the gospel! A great many are 20th century people, very much alive today, living entirely different lives from those they once knew. Fortunately, they applied the "heretical 'old-time religion' " before it was too late.

9

I acknowledge with thanks the help of many people who worked with me to make this book possible. Harry Saulnier, of course, gave many hours of his time. His secretary, Helen Koester, worked long hours on several occasions as she dug out needed material. Others on the Mission staff were gracious in helping me obtain information. I'm deeply indebted to Jack Odell and his "Unshackled!" staff for details relating to many converts of the Harry Saulnier era. Certain parts of early chapters of this book, particularly material relating to Harry Monroe and the Taylors, are based by permission on Carl Henry's Mission history, *A Doorway to Heaven*, published in 1942.

JAMES R. ADAIR

Chapter 1

SKID ROW, CHICAGO

DARKNESS WAS SETTLING softly over Chicago's Loop as I hurried from a restaurant on Wabash Avenue. A biting December wind, the kind that plays tag with you at every corner in Chicago, made me appreciate again the hot meal I had eaten. An el train clattered on the tracks above, and traffic on the street threaded its way by the steel beams supporting the el structure. From the corner of my eye I noticed a man move toward me from the shadows, and I turned instinctively. A thin wisp of a man, bent with sin more than with years, he fitted the role of a panhandler: gray stubble on his face; bleary eyes; threadbare, filthy clothes. I guessed he was in his 50's, though he looked older.

"Help me, Bud," he begged. "It's cold. I've got nowhere to go, and I haven't eaten today." He pulled his thin coat about him, hunching inside it, and looked up pathetically into my face.

Smelling whiskey on his breath, I shook my head. "Sorry, friend, but money isn't the solution to your problem. You'd only spend it on drink. You need to know Jesus Christ."

White anger flashed in the man's gaunt face. "Why, I bet I know more about the Bible than you do!" he said hotly, beginning to quote the account of the creation of man from Genesis.

"Fine," I told him, "but your knowledge is evidently in your head. When it gets in your heart, a change comes into your life."

Recommending a place where he could get help if he really wanted food and shelter, I turned to go. "Friend," I said, "I have a night class at Northwestern University. I must hurry on."

11

I stepped back as his expression suddenly changed. With a faraway look in his eyes, he muttered, *"Northwestern.* Why, I graduated from there." Then he named a prominent Chicago physician who he said was one of his classmates.

For a moment I looked at him. This derelict a university graduate? An M.D.? "But what happened?"

"Malpractice. An illegal operation. I was barred from practice—"

"—and then you took to drink," I added.

Sadness filled his eyes as I laid my hand on his bony shoulder. "There's no use being bitter," I said. "I know you're cold and hungry." Again I told him where he could get help. On an impulse, I took out a business card and scribbled on it, "Fix this man up." He, of course, didn't need the card to be received at the place, but I felt he'd appreciate it.

I walked north whispering a prayer against the wind that through a miracle old Doc would make a comeback and once again find a useful place in society. I had known of others who had. It could happen to Doc. I glanced back over my shoulder. He was shuffling south and turning the corner toward South State Street, clutching the card I had given him.

This episode occurred in the early 1950's, but I remember it well since it opened the door to Skid Row in a new way for me. Until I met Doc, I knew little or nothing of the anxiety and despair gnawing at the souls of these social outcasts. I had made my choices in life; they had made theirs. I was here; they were there. I had my world; they had theirs. We were worlds apart.

Yes, I was acquainted with the physical aspects of Chicago's vast Skid Row area. On occasion I had walked hurriedly through this twilight world, detouring around panhandlers if possible, always breathing a sigh of relief when I came again to sunshine.

Skid Row, Chicago, isn't all in one place; and it isn't always connected, though many derelicts wander from one Skid Row area to another. West Madison Street, North Clark, South State, and a few neighboring areas, all within a mile or two of the "world's busiest corner," State and Madison, look alike. You leave the business district with its towering buildings, banks, the stock exchange, and such famous name stores as Marshall Field's, Carsons, Wards, and Sears; and suddenly you are in this mysterious twilight world where Satan is paymaster.

Every third or fourth establishment seems to be a smelly, dark tavern blaring suggestive music and featuring beer on tap for 15 cents. Greasy restaurants and cafeterias vie for the Skid Row dollar with such signs as, "CHILI—LARGEST BOWL IN TOWN! 15¢" and "FULL SHOT AND A BEER, 25¢." Flophouses, posing as comfortable hotels, ask anywhere from 50 to 85 cents a night for chicken-wire cubicles. Your flesh crawls as you think of cockroaches, lice, and bedbugs. You quicken your step. Pawnshops offer to buy, sell, or exchange, and you instinctively know that many men have shuffled across the threshold to hock items they have found or stolen in order to get cash for more drink or dope. Employment agencies, called "slave markets" by the men, advertise for workers to come by at 6 A.M. for spot jobs. They boast that "everyday is payday."

On South State Street, just south of the elevated tracks, you enter an area called "Hell's Half Acre" before the turn of the century. Here for some years following the 1871 Chicago fire, after the city had been rebuilt and people were living it up again, the owner of the Lone Star Saloon got his name into the American common speech. Mickey Finn put his more affluent patrons to sleep before robbing them. Since then a knockout drop has been a "Mickey Finn."

In this area today the twilight world will be brightened by the new $2.5 million, six-story Jones Commercial High School building which was being constructed at the corner of State and Harrison when this book was written. But this is still Skid Row where tattoo parlors, taverns, pawnshops, and flophouses rub elbows with burlesque houses, movie theaters specializing in nudist colony films, and penny arcades with peep shows offering "Parisian movies for adults only." Pictures on the outside of the theaters lure high school boys, servicemen, and others who wander into the area. These pictures feature the feminine form as close to nature as the Municipal Code and the police will allow.

Since the evening I met Doc, the beggar from the shadows, I have sought to find the answers to many questions concerning the shuffling forms of humanity that inhabit Chicago's Skid Row areas. Is it a certain "type" of person who is served by Skid Row? Why do these men choose to live in cheap, vermin-infested flophouses? Why do they slouch for hours in semidark taverns, spending their last dime for beer or cheap wine and listening to a blaring juke box or a painted hussy singing suggestive songs? What has happened to men who, almost in the shadows of such famous hotels as the Palmer House and the Conrad Hilton, sleep under newspapers in an alley or doorway because they haven't even 50 cents for a flophouse bed or because they are too drunk to go farther?

Interviews with many of the men themselves and people who know them, plus other research, refuted any thoughts I had that there is a certain "type" person who frequents Skid Row. Actually, there are many types, and each type has a different combination of reasons for living in this twilight world. Statistics indicate that close to 15,000 homeless men haunt Chicago's Skid Row districts, having arrived by different routes, all victims of problems they couldn't control. Look them over and talk with some of them:

The elderly men watching TV in the lobby of the Ewing Hotel in the 700 block of South State are pensioners whose small monthly check won't allow them better living standards. They are without families, or their children no longer welcome them as members of the family. On Skid Row perhaps they find other men who understand them, and they can talk of the good old days.

Like the pensioner, the physically disabled man feels that Skid Row offers the best means of making his small monthly check meet his need for food, shelter, and clothing. Both he and the elderly pensioner can at least go to a mission if cash runs out before the month does. A lot of times it depends on such things as how often a man visits the taverns as to whether a check lasts a month.

The bewhiskered, dishevelled, bleary-eyed alcoholics, some of them once men of distinction like my friend Doc, find in Skid Row a place where their dollar will give them the maximum number of drinks and at the same time food and shelter. They have been rejected by normal society or have simply withdrawn and are frantically seeking to escape from reality. For some, absenteeism and drinking on the job separated them from well-paying positions.

In addition, you meet unskilled laborers and migrant workers seeking jobs in the slave market; the transient bums who beg for a living and move from place to place; the semisettled or settled panhandlers or other shiftless humanity who are physically able to work but choose not to; and a number of petty thieves, gamblers, confidence men, or other criminals hiding from the police.

To look into the lives of some of the residents of Skid Row, I spent an afternoon interviewing men on South State Street. I squared with each, telling him the purpose of my interview, and assuring him that real names would not be used. I asked each substantially the same questions and recorded their answers in their own words.

First, I interviewed "Bill," a bewhiskered man who smelled of beer and had blood on the front of a once-white shirt. His shirt was partly unbuttoned. Beneath it he wore unwashed long-handled underwear. Bill, who said he used to be a fundamentalist but now believed in reincarnation, told me he was 35; but he looked 45. Here, condensed, are comments he gave in reply to my questions:

"The place where I worked burned down, and I was out of a job. I came to St. Louis first, and somebody told me it was better around Chicago. It took me two days to hitchhike here. The first guy that picked me up was a colored guy. He gave me 50 cents and I got a sandwich with one quarter and beer with the other. Then another guy picked me up and took me about ten miles. I got a bunch of rides after that—I lost count. One guy picked me up and he had some whiskey. He said he was going to visit some cousins and he took me there and I slept the night on the floor.

"Then I got rides in cars and a couple of trucks to get to Chicago. Once a couple girls picked me up too—one was a WAC. I have a job washing dishes now—just enough to keep me going. Last night I stayed at the Eagle Hotel. I pay 80 cents a night there. Some floors have showers and some baths. Some of the fellows I meet are nice, and some are no good ———s. Some are good guys just like me who've been given bad breaks, guys who've tried to be somebody but can't because they can't get their chance."

I pointedly asked Bill why he drank.

"I don't know. I like it. I'm an alcoholic, I know that. It makes me feel good. It builds you up, settles your nerves. I took up the habit of smoking when I was 14. I started drinking back in my teen years but had to sneak around to do it because I wasn't 21. I'm a heavy drinker. I'm a beer drinker—whiskey and wine sometimes. The doctor told me I should drink tap beer if I must drink."

Next I talked with "Charlie," a thickset nervous man who said he was a laborer, 51 years of age:

"My occupation is factory work, cooking, cleaning. I'm a jack-of-all-trades. I live in a small hotel on Clark Street right now. My room isn't wonderful, but it's at least not on the street. It's chicken wire—you can lock it so people don't come in and bother you at night. I live in this area because of my financial situation. I usually work about 14 hours and get 9 dollars.

"I used to live with my brother here in Chicago, but things

didn't work out. I was married and divorced. I brought this situation on myself. I drink now because it's something I can't run away from. I drink mostly beer. After work I drink about a quart and a half."

"Arnold," who told me he was 65, impressed me immediately as a man much more refined and cultured than the other men to whom I had talked. Grandfatherly looking, balding and paunchy, he fumbled nervously through items in his billfold and at last found a paper which he proudly unfolded and showed me. It was an old tattered concert program in which he was featured as violinist. The picture was of a young man, but I could see the resemblance. A biographical sketch said that Arnold had studied in Europe. But why was he on South State Street, in seedy attire, minus his teeth?

"It's been quite a few years since I actually gave a concert. I haven't taught for years. I've had a few jobs but nothing significant."

Arnold revealed that his aged mother had, at his insistence, given him enough money to leave the area to get a fresh start at 65. Then, apparently to block his leaving, she took some of the money and hid it from him. Angry, he argued with her until she locked him out of the house, keeping him from his clothing, false teeth, and all else that he owned. Arnold was checking with a lawyer about filing suit against his mother.

My next interviewee introduced himself as "Clyde." A lanky fellow with sagging shoulders, he gave his age as 33. His front teeth were missing and he walked with a jump. He told me:

"I've been in Chicago since the first of September. I came here [from Indiana] to get a new start. I had an alcoholic problem, ended up in a state hospital, and they advised me to leave the state because I didn't have a chance in my hometown to make a comeback. I'm married and have three children. I'm not divorced, but I don't know where they are. The home got broken up because of drink. I was in the hospital altogether nine months.

"I came up here and it hasn't seemed to help me. When I first came here, I got a job; and I got drunk and messed up my job. I've been taking about one spot job a week. The fellows on Skid Row are nice—I haven't had any trouble with them. But I'd like to get off this area. The thing I want most in the world is to get off this area, I can tell you that. But I haven't got any friends in the world. People treat us like dogs. We'll be standing on the street and people will ride by and stare out the car like we're animals. I hope that I'll get away from here eventually."

"Jim," 54, a coal-black Negro, had an equally hard-luck story:

"St. Louis is my hometown. I've been here two years. I don't like it around here. I don't know why I live here. I came on a freight train with another fellow. He robbed me, or at least he got me robbed. My wife is dead. I stay here because of the missions when I'm not working. I depend mainly on spot jobs I can pick up. I do mostly kitchen work. [Where I live] it's dirty. You can't fasten the doors. I watch TV in the lobby. You can't go in after 10. You can get out at 5 in the morning, but you don't have to go out until 7. When I'm not working, I sit around. I can drink or leave it. I took my last drink a month ago. It doesn't make any difference whether I have anything or not. I think the missions do a lot for the people. If it weren't for the missions I don't know what all these guys would do. I wouldn't know where I was."

"Ed," a light-complexioned Negro with a moustache and bushy hair, told me he was 28, a drifter half his life. His clothing was typical of the street. Polite and conversant, he said:

"My hometown is Philadelphia. I've been drifting from place to place. I had a chance to go to Las Vegas, but I was short of money. My work is generally restaurant. I work sometimes at Goldblatt's. This morning I was five minutes late, so I had to forget all about the Goldblatt's bus. We wash cars for them.

"I'm a light drinker. I drink beer, wine. Beer is 25 cents. In the course of a month I guess I would spend anywhere in the neighborhood of 36 or 39 bucks. The reason I stay around here is because I can get back and forth to work. I don't particularly like the area, but as it stands so far I have no other alternative."

"George," minus three lower teeth, slouched sickly as he talked surlily and nervously rubbed sores on his face:

"I'll be 48 in February. Chicago is my hometown. I have been a chemist by occupation. I was in charge of the research department at ——————. The last I worked at my occupation was seven or eight years ago—since my divorce. The divorce threw me for a loop. I turned alcoholic. I never touched a drink or smoked a cigarette either, even though my father had a tavern. My problem was gambling. Gambling broke up my home. Then I began to rely more and more on liquor. I can outdrink 16 men. I drink Scotch, whiskey, beer, wine. I'm a compulsive drinker. I'm an escapist, trying to escape from reality, you see. I try to escape my problems and forget my past. I drink and drink until I get so sick I can't look at the stuff. Then I got to lay off of it; I can't eat; I can't hold water. It's a vicious circle.

"I couldn't even count what I spend a month on liquor. My grandfather left me 175,000 dollars, and I ran through that in two years just in gambling. I get to the point where money doesn't mean anything. I always had anything I wanted, new cars and all.

"There are a lot of hotels around here that have the cages. You run into bed bugs and conditions of that short. Misery loves company, and that's the first thing I like about this area. When you're miserable you like to find a fellow as miserable as you are.

"Naturally, the missions are needed. I don't get tired of hearing the messages. I have read the Bible over several times. I had six courses of religion in Loyola University. We had to go to communion every Friday or we were fined one dollar. I was a Catholic, but my wife was German Lutheran."

One drifter I talked with had an ugly gash in his forehead

that had just begun to heal. A short, balding man who had the marks of being more than the 39 years he claimed, "Fred" said he was a painter, that Racine, Wisconsin, was his hometown. As we talked, I ultimately learned how he had suffered the head injury:

"The rooms at the flophouse I live in are like a birdcage— screen on the top. I think the reason this place is quieter is because most of the men work in the slave markets or labor pools, and they're tired; and the hotel don't allow too much rough housing. I've been depending on the slave markets mainly in the past few weeks. But I find it pretty hard getting a job now when they see this gash on my head.

"I was a victim of circumstances. I couldn't sleep one night for the bedbugs, so I just started walking the street. I had been drinking the night before. I was sitting in Sophie's Restaurant down State Street. This was a week ago this morning. I was sitting there drinking coffee looking through the mirror at this guy who had his girl friend with him. He figured I was eyeing her up. So he clobbered me with a stool. I went to the hospital and they took X rays and taped it up. The cops took me there.

"I started drinking when I was in World War II. I couldn't really say why I drink. I was married and we had a divorce, and I guess I just kept on drinking. I'd go on a binge and then lose a good job. I'd stay off it for a couple, three weeks and then be back at it. It's a vicious cycle. I just keep on going one day to the next. I drink mostly beer, whiskey, and when you get broke you start on cheap wine. This is about 50 cents a pint. I'm a heavy drinker. I know I spend 40 to 50 dollars a month on liquor."

I talked to "Tim," who has been around Skid Row for many years and asked about crime and evil conditions in general in the area, particularly along South State. Among other things, he said:

"Shove a dollar bill over the counter in a tavern, and you'll get your head split open for the change. You see a lot of jack-rolling. They get you around the neck, hold your arms in back, and go through your pockets. It's usually two guys working together. Sometimes somebody will pick a fight to get at you. Maybe a bartender points out a guy with money because he's going to get a percentage. I've seen them rob guys on the street in broad daylight. After dark, guys usually will walk right on the curb to stay away from the buildings because they'll pull you into a doorway so fast, one on each side and one behind you with a knife."

"I learned about these things the hard way," another man, "Jake," told me. "I was a merchant marine, and when I came to Chicago two years ago I had two big checks on me. I ate my breakfast in a restaurant and cashed a check for about 150 dollars. On North Clark Street I walked into the King's Palace and sat there drinking. When I walked outside, I felt myself getting dizzy and sick; and all I know is the lights went out. When I woke up, my money, wallet, identification papers, and all were gone. Another time on Madison I got hit too."

Dope props up the spirits of a large percentage of Skid Row inhabitants, one man guessing that 65 percent of the men use dope in one form or another. Other estimates, however, are much lower.

"Some men," Tim told me, "sell medicinal stuff that they get from the hospitals, or they'll get prescriptions from a county doctor and sell the prescriptions to somebody who really wants the pills. Then the guy who was to use it for a pain killer in his own body goes out and buys a gallon of wine with the money.

"They got what they call 'pushers' on the street. Red Devil is a popular form of dope, something like phenobarbital to quiet your nerves. You take quite a few of them and take wine also and that makes you higher than a kite. A marihuana cigarette is 50 cents a stick or 10 dollars a pack. Those on dope usually start with marihuana, then lose their kick and take heroin. After they shoot the vein, there's no hope."

I asked "Tim" about some of the notorious joints along South
State.

"The biggest one on State Street was Boots' Tavern until it
was torn down 18 months ago [to make way for the new Jones
Commercial High School]. Anything could happen in there.
It was patronized by police officers also. Lots of times I was
thrown out the back door for drinking a guy's shot while he
was watching TV, or something like that. The bartender himself would throw you out. Boots was quite a man. If he'd tell
you to leave and you didn't move fast enough, he'd throw you
out. He's opened a place on Madison now, a block towards
Des Plaines.

"The Show Boat is a notorious one, along with the 666 Club
and the 700 Club. They're after-hour places. The 700 Club is
a call house—if you want a girl you call the Show Boat and
meet them in the 700 Club and go from there. Skid Row men
don't often go there; they make a few nickels by spotting customers. It used to be if you wanted to know anything you'd ask
a cab driver, but now ask a bum on Skid Row and he'll let you
know what's happening because he gets around. You can't get
in the 666 Club unless the attendant knows you. You don't get
in unless you push the buzzer on his door. If you don't look good
to him, he won't let you in."

In this twilight world of Skid Row, festering with disease,
crawling with cockroaches and bedbugs, reeking with the sicken-
ing smell of cheap wine and beer, writhing with dope, there
looms a light of hope, a place where the burdened can find rest
—and God. It's just north of the 666 Club on South State—
but unlike the Club, the door is always open.

Chapter 2

THE OLD LIGHTHOUSE

FILTHY DIRTY, unshaven, and sick, Ben Engstrom, 55-year-old former electrical foreman at the United States Steel Company Mill, Gary, Indiana, quivered as the white-jacketed doctor checked him over. From Skid Row's twilight world, Ben had been admitted to Cook County Hospital, a sprawling charity institution on Chicago's near West Side. Drink, which had ended his career at the steel mill, now threatened his very existence.

Looking into Ben's bleary eyes, the doctor leveled with his patient. "Engstrom, your only hope is extensive therapy. We'll arrange to admit you to an institution where you can get the best psychiatric care."

For an instant the patient's brain—virtually pickled with alcohol—reeled, and he remembered a scene of three years before. Walking aimlessly down South State Street, just south of the Loop, he had stopped at the busy corner of Harrison and State to hear a tall, handsome, broad-shouldered man making a sidewalk speech.

"Take electricity, for example," the man boomed. "Have you actually seen it? Do you understand it completely? No. Yet you have faith in it. You know that it will give you light at only a flick of a switch. God is like that. You don't see Him, but He's waiting for you to reach out to Him. All you need to do is call on Him, tell Him of your need. Trust Jesus Christ, and it will be like pushing a switch—your life will be flooded with light. You'll be born again and saved from the old life."

Moments later the speaker, Harry Saulnier, superintendent of the nearby Pacific Garden Mission, put a compassionate arm around Ben's drooping shoulder. He urged him to confess his need to God and to reach out and receive salvation and by faith trust God to make his life new.

Just the fact that Saulnier knew something about electricity gave Ben, the former electrical foreman, a feeling of kinship to this big man. Soon he bowed his head at Saulnier's suggestion and tried to please his new friend by saying words to God that were supposed to work a miracle in his life. But nothing happened. Ben returned to his old way of life, wandering Skid Row, begging, borrowing, stealing drinks. Seemingly he would exist here a few more years, then join other unfortunates in "potter's field." Or, if he was lucky, maybe his sister would bury him.

Now, three years later, in March 1945, the face of Harry Saulnier came into focus in the foggy mind of alcoholic Ben. "Please, Doc," the patient blubbered, "I want to try something else first. I know where I can get help, if I can only get there. I'd like to see Harry Saulnier at the Pacific Garden Mission on South State Street."

The doctor gave Ben streetcar fare and wished him well. An hour later, seeking the one man he believed could help him, Ben walked into the Mission, remained for the evening service, then walked to the prayer room to talk and pray with Saulnier. This time, like Pilgrim of old, he knelt in faith at the foot of the cross and lost his burden of sin. After his encounter with the almighty Son of God, Ben walked from the prayer room with hope surging in his bosom.

That night, because there was no room left in the Mission dorm, Ben was sent to a nearby hotel where he slept soundly for the first time in months. The next morning the day seemed brighter, the air purer as Ben rolled from his cot and joined other Skid Row men who had come into the Mission to escape the chill March winds. A Mission attendant gave him clean clothing and invited him to a Bible study for new converts before breakfast.

Though still in a weakened physical condition, Ben had to pinch himself, for he still felt like a new person. And the man who led the Bible study kept emphasizing this very fact: "You have been born again. You have a new life. Christ is now your life. He is in your heart, giving you new desires. You have been born into God's very own family. Listen what John 1:12 says: 'But as many as received him [Christ], to them gave he power to become the sons of God, even to them that believe on his name.' Walk today, and everyday, with your Saviour. He will never let you down."

Later, with four one-dollar bills in his pocket, Ben tested his new spiritual legs in a walk along South State. It had been nearly 24 hours since he had had a drink. The smell of beer from a tavern met his nostrils. His ear caught the sounds of the bar: the clinking of glasses, the babble of men slumped on stools.

Ben Engstrom stood there a minute—maybe two. Then resolutely he turned and walked to his warm new home, the Old Lighthouse.

Though he's had other battles in which drink sought to recapture him, today Ben Engstrom, a silver-haired man bearing the wrinkles of 76 years, is one of thousands of trophies of grace of the modern era of the old Pacific Garden Mission where God has been rescuing men and women from the brink of hell since 1877. Ben himself continues to live at the Old Lighthouse where he has served as building engineer for 21 years. He delights in telling how God, in grace, mercy and mighty power, redeemed him from the gutter and made him a citizen of heaven. I can see him now in a Mission meeting, an air of dignity about him, holding his silvery head high and his shoulders back, telling men of the street the story that never grows old to him.

Miracles as thrilling as that of Ben Engstrom are repeated time and again at 650 State Street, dubbed "A Doorway to Heaven" many years ago. Annually, in past years, as many as 10,000 persons have walked to the prayer rooms of Pacific

Garden Mission and made professions of faith in Jesus Christ. The Mission firmly believes that this is the only hope for a real comeback, based on II Corinthians 5:17, a Bible verse often used as a sermon text at PGM: "If any man be in Christ, he is a new creature: old things are passed away; behold, all things are become new."

Today the Mission, second oldest in the United States, is one of the largest and most efficient institutions of its kind. It was here I sent Doc, the erstwhile physician who helped introduce me to the Skid Row the Mission serves. Housed in four buildings, the Pacific Garden Mission serves not only Skid Row derelicts like Doc and the Ben Engstrom of yesteryear but GI's, destitute families, and up-and-outers who find their way here for spiritual counsel. In addition, the light from the Old Lighthouse beams out across the U.S.—and many parts of the world—through films, books, and an expertly produced dramatic radio series, "Unshackled!" The program featuring true stories of Mission converts, is broadcast over 205 radio stations in the U.S. and 25 foreign countries. Annually hundreds report that the broadcast has brought them into vital contact with Jesus Christ.

For nearly a century Pacific Garden Mission has welcomed an estimated six million persons, and only heaven's records list the great host of those who met the Saviour there. Executives, lawyers, doctors, and scientists have joined cooks, sailors, common panhandlers, and crooks in walking down the aisle as audiences have burst into singing such familiar invitation songs as "Just As I Am" and "Jesus, I Come."

"Everlastingly at it," a slogan coined and made famous by Mel Trotter at the mission he founded in Grand Rapids, Michigan, typifies the Old Lighthouse on South State. When the day staff isn't on duty counseling and winning souls, the night staff is throwing out the lifeline. Figuratively, the door never closes. In summer and winter, in sweltering heat and bitter cold, doormen stand on the sidewalk from 8 A.M. till 10:30 P.M. distributing gospel tracts and inviting passers-by inside. If a GI needs a bunk at 2 A.M., the night man welcomes him and tucks him in. Or if a woman seeking shelter rings the bell of the Women's Division, she is taken in and given care by a member of the staff of that busy wing of the Mission.

From the early days of the Mission, gospel services have been the backbone of the ministry. For many years three services have been held daily—one in the morning, one at noon, the other in the evening. Full houses of some 350 people are not uncommon, especially on Saturday nights when visitors from many churches gather with Skid Row men and women for a two-hour song and testimony service.

Not long ago I looked in on a rousing Saturday evening testimony meeting, pencil and notebook in hand. A group of junior high young people from Wheaton (Ill.) Bible Church provided the special music. With Harry Saulnier leading, the crowded mission hall became a corner of heaven as one after another stood and told what Christ had done for him.

"Make them short. No preaching. Just tell simply what Christ means to you!" Saulnier urged graciously.

But some of the testimonies were long, and a few preached. They were old-timers, full and burdened for those in the audience to share what they had discovered in Christ. Short testimonies from new converts were given timidly. Amens rang out time and again.

A thickset man in the front row told the audience that he had once come to the Mission with his wife. An alcoholic, he had listened to the gospel and returned home under conviction. Later, back at the Mission, he went to the prayer room and was saved and delivered from drink. "I call this the 'House of Miracles!'" he bellowed. "Here Christ delivered me from sin and drink."

A woman of perhaps 60 testified that God had saved her at home 32 years ago as she read the Word. A man with a built-in PA system said he had "trailed the devil for 48 years like the tail of a comet." He had met Christ, and his life had been changed in a split second.

The crowd listened eagerly as a small girl came to the pulpit and recited Psalm 23. Someone told me that her mother had been on the verge of giving up when she visited PGM and found the Lord.

Busloads of church folk, oldsters and young people alike, come from hundreds of miles away, visit the Old Lighthouse regularly and invariably go away fired up over what they see and hear. A church in Albion, Indiana, reported: "We truly were blessed visiting your Mission. Everybody feels the same. Many testimonies at church on Thursday and Sunday nights verified the blessings we received being in your service that evening."

A representative of a Chicago area church was blessed through serving: "One of the teen-age boys I brought received Christ. My assistant led a man to Christ in the counseling room. I talked to one man but don't think he was really under conviction, and a young man we talked with outside the Mission received Christ. Now we've got another group that wants to come this Saturday."

PGM deputation workers carry the fire and spirit of the soul-winning ministry to distant points, challenging church members to win souls and exhorting the unsaved to come to Christ. In one recent year, teams preached to more than 45,000 people and saw 1171 profess Christ as Saviour.

Back at the Old Lighthouse the some 80 staff members—personal workers, secretaries, office workers, doormen, receptionists—together with the superintendent and department directors pray fervently at several daily separate sessions asking God for a great harvest of souls. And because of their prayers, and those of countless thousands elsewhere, God blesses with souls daily.

A policeman brought a man to the Mission at 2:30 one June morning. Though the dormitory was closed and filled with sleeping men, the night man greeted the stranger and took him to the Servicemen's Center for a snack and coffee. He slept in a chair the remainder of the night. Before he left, he was able to say:

"Right here at the Mission the miracle happened. I recovered my fellowship with the Lord Jesus! How good it was to experience His love and guidance again. Now I am living for Him. I know that without Him I would be nothing."

A World War II veteran who had promised God in North Africa, in the heat of battle, that he would live for Him wandered into the Mission not long ago, a pitiful wreck of a man. He had failed to keep his promise when he returned and had resumed a machine shop business. Ultimately, because of drink, he lost the business. Then his wife and three children were killed in an automobile accident. This sent him into a drunken tailspin, and for 18 months he was a Skid Row wanderer. In the Mission he placed his faith in Christ and before he left he announced:

"I know that God has forgiven my sins and saved me, and I am going back home to Wildwood, New Jersey, to the parents that loved me and prayed for me."

"Except for the souls the Lord of the harvest so graciously gives, Pacific Garden Mission would be merely another social service organization," explains Superintendent Saulnier. "But the cooks prepare some 600 meals a day for a purpose. Some 285 beds are made daily for Skid Row men, GI's, and women and children for one primary purpose. The four buildings are kept spic and span with one aim in mind. That precious souls might be won!"

At the Old Lighthouse personal workers look upon every man as a precious soul for whom Christ died, and they desperately want to communicate the gospel to such men. Likewise, women personal workers deal tenderly with homeless mothers and fallen women of the street. Through such dedicated workers the Holy Spirit works to transform those who have lost all hope because of the weight of sin upon them.

At the Old Lighthouse it's all part of the fruitful soul-winning ministry begun in 1877 because God gave two humble, unlikely people a tremendous burden for salvaging human wrecks by courageously beaming the blessed gospel light to them on Skid Row, Chicago!

Chapter 3

TELEGRAM FROM THE ROCKIES

THE DAY DAWNED bright and clear that late summer in 1877 in the small Colorado mining town where Colonel George Clarke, a stocky, balding, middle-aged man, was about to close a real estate deal. Ordinarily he would have been happy, for the deal promised him a substantial profit. Even being temporarily on business in Colorado, away from Chicago and the slums where his wife had been dragging him to visit the poor, should have made the colonel's heart sing.

However, that wasn't the case. As the Colorado day progressed, thunder growled beyond the snowcapped peaks, threatening a storm. But already lightning flashed within the colonel's heart, and each flash revealed the delicate features of his wife— and the haggard outcasts she wanted to help. In a growing way this tiny woman he had married four years earlier was giving her time and energy to visiting and ministering to unfortunates. During the Civil War, in which Clarke had risen to lieutenant colonel with the 13th Illinois Volunteers, she had started a little mission Sunday school at the corner of State and 23rd Streets to reach the poor for God. This wasn't so bad. After all, he himself had been helping. But now Sarah was praying about starting a mission to minister the gospel of Christ to drunkards and other derelicts along the levee—the stretch of South Clark Street from Van Buren to 22nd Street, near the Chicago River.

His real estate deal forgotten, Colonel Clarke talked long with God on his knees as he pondered his problem. "O God, You know I love You, and I want to do what is right and good

in Your sight. You know what a mess I make of preaching and
how my heart aches for the miserable people dear Sarah wants
to reach. Show me, O Lord, what I must do, and give me power
to do Your blessed will."

Right here in the Rockies several years earlier Clarke had
wrestled with God concerning the salvation of his soul. About
to transact a shady land deal, he had remembered the prayers
of his saintly mother and broke before the Lord. Confessing
his sin and need of forgiveness, he had felt the cleansing stream
from the Saviour's Cross and from that time had counted himself a member of God's family.

Now he wanted definite directions from his heavenly Father.
Somehow he felt like a runaway boy out here dabbling again in
real estate while Sarah continued the work among the people of
the levee. Finally, the storm over, George Clarke lifted his head
and looked unto the mountains and above to the blue sky. "Yes,
Lord, I'll give You my life and will preach the gospel to the
people of the levee. I'll trust You to give me the ability."

A short time later the town telegraph operator began tapping
out a message. The exact wording of the message Sarah Dunn
Clarke got that day in 1877 in Chicago was never recorded,
though in substance it read: "Plans changed. God wants me to
join you in starting a mission. George." Tears in her eyes and
a glow in her heart, Sarah whispered a thank you to God and
began to think about the best place for a mission.

The catastrophic Chicago fire in 1871 had sent most churches
to the city's outskirts, so a gospel work was desperately needed
in the area now infested with gambling halls, saloons, and
brothels. But where would God have them begin this counter-
attack against sin? Sarah Clarke wondered.

The decision would await George's return from Colorado.
Meantime she would pray for God's wisdom and leading.

Mrs. Clarke had been in the habit of taking matters to God
for a good many years, though it had been in only comparatively

recent times that she had felt God's closeness to her and His power throbbing and working in her life.

Born November 13, 1835, in New York's Cayuga County, she grew up in a Christian atmosphere. Attending Sunday school, she was taught to abstain from card playing, dancing, and theater attendance. But not until she was 20 did she really have a personal encounter with God. A friend sensed her need of knowing the Saviour personally, and returning from the Wilkes-Barre Seminary and standing on the platform of the Scranton depot, the friend asked Sarah Dunn to give her heart to God. This prompted her to place her trust in Jesus Christ for her salvation, and a desire was kindled in her heart to please God through her life.

But another encounter with God was to change the course of her life. After teaching school in Elmira, New York, she moved in 1861 to Waterloo, Iowa, and here continued faithfully attending church. But God dealt with her in her home to prepare her for the ministry He would lead her into later in Chicago.

One day Sarah Dunn was putting the finishing touches on an elaborate decoration for the family home. As she paused to admire the work, it seemed that an audible voice spoke to her: "What are you doing to decorate your heavenly home?"

Thoughts of perishing souls marching to a Christless eternity flooded Sarah's mind as she pondered this penetrating question. Time, she reasoned, was a precious gift from God—in reality it was God's time, not hers, since she belonged to Him. "Why should I spend priceless time on earthly adornments when souls need to be won for the Master? Surely this is the way I can adorn my heavenly mansion through all the cycles of eternity."

From this time on, her consuming passion in life was the winning of sinners to Jesus Christ and spending her time in the service of her Master. Even when she moved to Chicago and sought to make fashionable calls to assure her social standing, her conscience wouldn't let her continue. So, wearing simple clothing, she began visiting needy families and ministering to both their spiritual and material needs.

Shortly it dawned on Sarah that this was God's calling in life for her.

In 1869, with the aid of several friends, she opened her mission Sunday school at State and 23rd. During the early days of the school, in a business transaction, she met Colonel George Clarke. Two years after the Chicago fire they were married.

The colonel, like Mrs. Clarke, was a native of New York state, having been born in Ostego county on February 22, 1827. He had studied at Beloit College, Beloit, Wisconsin, and became one of its first graduates. He then became the principal of the Milton Academy. Later he edited a paper called the *Sauk County Standard* and, after studying law, was admitted to the bar in 1853. Finally, his interests turned to real estate and business took him to Colorado, where he had his first encounter with God. His first wife perished in the Chicago fire.

Following his second marriage in 1873, wanting both to please God and the tiny woman who had become his wife, Colonel Clarke assisted in the Sunday school mission. He tried occasionally to preach, and he gradually learned the lesson of giving to the Lord—diverting funds to "the Lord's treasury" once earmarked for Cuban cigars and the entertainment of friends.

But not until he wrestled with the Lord in Colorado the second time did he decide that ministering the Word to the unfortunates of Chicago was to be his task for the remainder of his life.

On September 15, 1877, the Clarkes put the finishing touches on their work in a tiny store at 386 South Clark Street, virtually next door to a notorious place called Hinky Dink's, and spread the word that they would have services that evening. It was the first rescue mission west of Jerry McAuley's Water Street Mission in New York, at that time the nation's only other mission. If the Clarkes were aware of this work, there is no record of it.

‒ "Colonel Clarke's Mission," as it was known in its early days, featured a wheezy organ and the unpolished but fervent preaching of the colonel himself. As he talked to noisy, restless crowds, made up of drunks, dope addicts, harlots, and thieves, tears trickled down the colonel's cheeks. More often than not, he preached on his favorite text, John 3:16: "God so loved the world."

Seating capacity of the Mission was about 40 when the audience crowded together on the backless, wooden benches. A potbellied stove kept out the Chicago chill; kerosene lamps supplied flickering light; and heartwarming Bible quotations graced the walls. Behind the table from which Colonel Clarke preached, a large sign proclaimed, "GOD IS LOVE." A warning on the left wall, "THOU GOD SEEST ME," was contrasted with the invitation on the right wall, "COME UNTO ME, ALL YE THAT LABOUR AND ARE HEAVY LADEN, AND I WILL GIVE YOU REST."

"Saloons on either side, with their banjos and accompanying instruments, were a great combination," penned Mother Clarke in describing the opening of the Mission. "However, we held the fort—Mr. Clarke preached, and I tried to keep crooked men straight.

"But such a coming and going was never seen before. Order— heaven's 'first law'—had never been injected in their minds, and it took the wisdom of Solomon to separate the drunken men and keep that crowd in order."

Despite the confusion, God honored the preaching of His Word, and during the first days four professed Christ as Saviour, three going on to give outward evidence of changed lives. In three years in the tiny Mission on the South Clark Street levee, the old, old story of Jesus and His love and power moved the hearts of hundreds. Night after night, as the colonel pleaded from his table at the front and Mrs. Clarke moved tenderly among the audience, God loosed Satan's chains from harlots, burglars, drunkards, and other patrons of brothels, gambling joints, and opium dens.

Then came the day in 1880 when Colonel Clarke went hunting for larger quarters. His nose for a good deal in real estate, now consecrated to God, led him finally to a building recently vacated by the notorious Pacific Beer Garden, "a place where the vilest and toughest were accustomed to come for cheap beer . . . the most murderous joint west of New York City." Here the Colonel rented a sizable room. The new address was 100 East Van Buren Street (later, in 1909, changed to 67 West Van Buren, when Chicago changed its numbering system). Near the southwest corner of Van Buren and what is now Federal Street, the Mission put out the welcome mat to the countless sinners who patronized the dens of iniquity that made the area a festering sore in Chicago's backyard.

Proclaiming the Mission as "the greatest on earth" and occasionally fishing there for souls himself, Dwight L. Moody, fresh from evangelistic meetings in England, urged the Clarkes to advertise to the world that the old Pacific Beer Garden had been transformed. "Just strike out the word *beer* and add the word *mission*," he advised.

Thus, "Colonel Clarke's Mission" became the "Pacific Garden Mission," a name destined to become world famous as God was about to add to the list of converts some men who would herald the same glad news of Christ far beyond Chicago's Skid Row.

Chapter 4

COLONEL AND "MOTHER" CLARKE'S CHILDREN

AFTER THE CLARKES LEASED for God the area once occupied by the notorious Pacific Beer Garden, they threw themselves into the work with even greater ardor, resulting in an endless stream of gloriously transformed lives. They never had children of their own but, in a real sense, these were their children. Many of them in later years tenderly called Mrs. Clarke "Mother." The Spirit of the living God was honoring the simple gospel messages preached faithfully night after night by the colonel and others who came to assist in the ministry of fishing for men.

Over the door a sign proclaimed, "HOPE FOR ALL WHO ENTER," and day and night the Clarkes tried desperately to convey this message to drunkards, outcasts, and others who crept in from the surrounding world of barrooms, opium dives, gambling establishments, and red-light houses.

The first of a line of famous converts of Pacific Garden Mission gave Colonel Clarke a hard time the night he came to Christ in 1880. Harry Monroe had just been released by a federal judge in Detroit from a counterfeiting charge. Hitting Chicago, he automatically entered a saloon and ordered a schooner of beer. As he lifted the glass, he suddenly stopped. *If I drink this,* he thought, *I'm right back where I was.*

He shoved the glass back toward the bartender and stalked out. Moments later, passing the Mission, he heard music. Twenty-seven-year-old Harry Monroe pushed open the door, stood there for a moment, then sat down. As the meeting closed, Colonel Clarke approached Monroe and asked him to accept Jesus.

"You stick to your business, and I'll stick to mine," the thickset Monroe fired back.

The big-hearted colonel did stick to his business, for he sensed that the message delivered that evening by D. W. Potter, a prominent Chicago banker, had brought conviction to the heart of the hardened young man. "Young man, do you know that Jesus loves you and so do I?"

Monroe trembled as the Mission superintendent told him how the blood of Jesus could wipe away all of the sin of his soul and how God could give him a wonderful new start.

Moments later a penitent Harry Monroe was talking to the heavenly Father. "I quit booze from this minute on," he blurted. "God be merciful to me, a sinner, and save me for Jesus' sake."

That night the Colonel put Harry up in a cheap room, since in those days the Mission did not have dormitory space. For the first time in 12 years, Harry wrote to his mother back in Massachusetts, sharing with her the glory that filled his bosom.

The next day, Sunday, he gave his first testimony in the Mission. Within a few weeks, after the Colonel discovered his ability to sing, Harry was given charge of the song services and helped make the Mission hall throb with glad gospel songs that became strong competition for the tinny banjo music drifting from the barrooms nearby. Unknown to Harry Monroe at the time, it was God's way of training him for a great ministry as the next superintendent of the Old Lighthouse.

Though they worked long hours and faced times when they weren't sure how they would pay their bills, the Clarkes never let discouragement cross their threshold. In a brief history of the Mission written 37 years after they flung open the doors of the Old Lighthouse, Mother Clarke wrote that the word *discouragement* "was never in our vocabulary." In her cursory style, she penned this illustration:

"In the early history of the Mission . . . a dummy train conveyed us . . . [to] our home [in Morgan Park on Chicago's South Side] . . .

"[We] had been tramping in the rain and slush all day, taking our late train as usual, at the midnight hour, obliged then to walk nearly two miles from the train to our home, in a terrific storm, facing a heavy sleeting hail and rain all the way. Entering the house [we] found his satanic majesty on hand, and with a slight [tap] on the shoulder, and with a modest voice [he] said, 'Does it pay?'

" 'Yes,' I very emphatically replied, 'I'd walk ten miles—or all night—if I could be the means of winning a soul.'

"That insinuation never accosted us again. *Disappointments* have been many. But discouragement *never*."

Their secret, of course, lay in the fact that their lives were wholly wrapped up in serving God and helping and loving the people to whom He had sent them to minister. It was no 9:00 to 5:00 job and then home for a quiet evening. On his sixty-third birthday Colonel Clarke, in a lengthy poem written to Mrs. Clarke, put it in these terms:

> Not oft we've sat around our hearth,
> On winter's stormy night,
> To look upon the glowing coals,
> Of fires burning bright,
> But trust we've brought to darken'd hearts,
> A little more of light.

In bringing the gospel to the people of the twilight world of their day, the Clarkes practiced sacrifice in the strictest sense of the word. During their society days when Colonel Clarke's business know-how gave them a good income, they had lived on a level expected of well-to-do people. But, with their income reduced considerably as Colonel Clarke gave himself wholly to the work of the Mission, they found it harder and harder to produce ready cash to keep the Lighthouse door open.

At times when finances were at an ebb, Mrs. Clarke wrote, "We had a rich Father and we trusted Him. 'He who marks the sparrow's fall' has always shielded us in times of storm."

Determined not to close the Mission door to any needy person, the Clarkes went to their knees on many occasions. Once God met a financial obligation through a miracle as thrilling and wonderful to the Clarkes as was the miracle of the manna from heaven to the children of Israel. And, indeed, the 19th century miracle was not a great deal unlike the one of Old Testament days. Mrs. Clarke described it in these terms:

"Next morning . . . we beheld our home garden nearly covered with mushrooms (a little in advance of the season) and when they were gathered and prepared for market, sold for a sufficient income to replace the expenditures of the previous night. No mushrooms were ever seen there before. Nor any since."

The mushrooms were sold to the then already famous Palmer House in downtown Chicago. Little did patrons that night know they were eating heavenly food.

God seemed to speak to the Clarkes about "indulgences of former years [that] could be disposed of. So," related the Mission mother, "we placed *all* on the altar—all of our jewelry, of every description, diamonds, and other valued presents (with associations too sacred to mention)—all alike was given to the Lord, for His cause—and for souls."

The Lord blessed this consecration, for soon Colonel Clarke was given opportunity to invest in a mining operation that increased their income so that they had few financial problems for ten years.

But even with this additional security, the Clarkes didn't change. Their bankbook belonged to God. If there were no funds in the Mission account to pay a bill, Mother Clarke immediately wrote a personal check.

Twice a week Colonel Clarke "held the fort" alone as the Mission mother visited jail prisoners or patients in the County

Hospital. God gave many souls as the tiny woman stopped and talked to prisoners and patients as if they were her own sons and daughters.

On a sultry Sunday afternoon, August 7, 1880, Mrs. Clarke greeted the guard cheerily at Cook County Jail. As he opened the heavy barred door for her, he commented, "It's sure a scorcher. Wouldn't have blamed you for taking this afternoon off." Mother Clarke, assuring him that she had to be about her Father's business despite the weather, trotted on to talk to the men behind the bars of the cells.

In cell 79 she saw "one of the most forlorn, discouraged, brokenhearted specimens of humanity eyes ever looked upon." Mrs. Clarke, less than five feet tall and wearing a little pancake hat, looked out of place as she stood there quietly pleading with the prisoner to look to God for cleansing and a new start. Soon the man fell to his knees and sobbed out his story to God, asking His forgiveness and the new life He offered.

"This man developed into a marvelous Christian character," Mrs. Clarke wrote. "Loyalty, love, and devotion seemed to be the dominant Christian graces controlling his life." For 24 years he served the Lord until his death in June 1912.

One of the most colorful children of the Clarkes was a 71-year-old man who became known after his conversion as "Sunshine" Harris. Claiming to be an infidel, he was a drunkard for 50 years. Occasionally he came into the Mission to antagonize the workers. Colonel Clarke often pleaded with him to begin anew with Jesus, but Harris returned to the streets, picking up cigarette butts to satisfy the awful craving for tobacco that he had. Finally, in August 1899, he bought a Testament, and the first words he read were, "Thou fool, this night thy soul shall be required of thee" (Luke 12:20). Angry, he laid the Testament down, but a few nights later he went to the Mission and raised both hands for prayer.

"I was assisted by a Christian lady to the altar; and when I called upon the Lord, He heard my cry. And the load of sin

mountain high rolled off," Harris later testified. "I rose to my
feet and exclaimed, 'Thanks be to God for His unspeakable gift
and for Pacific Garden Mission!' "

He returned to his room that night and thoroughly house-
cleaned, discarding bottles of whiskey and beer, pipes, tobacco,
and cards and putting in their place an open Bible. For eight
years, until his death in 1907, Harris spread sunshine wherever
he went, often testifying in the Mission of his life-changing
encounter with Christ.

"Jimmy the Rat," an Indiana farm boy, was a trophy of grace
that Mrs. Clarke often pointed to as an example of the mighty
power of God to unshackle a person from the worst sort of
habit. Jimmy at sixteen fell victim to dope and three years later
became a prisoner, living a ratlike existence, in an opium den
near the Mission. Once he heard a group from the Mission
holding a street meeting and singing, "I am so glad that Jesus
loves me, Jesus loves even me." He started out of the opium den
but was dragged back.

Finally one day, Jimmy was beaten and left unconscious on a
pile of lumber. Rain and the fresh air revived Jimmy, and he
made his way to the Mission. He started up the aisle, holding
up both hands and calling out, "I want somebody to pray for
me!"

Mrs. Clarke came quietly from the platform and put her hand
on his arm and led him to a front seat. When she knelt, he
dropped on his knees beside her. That night Jimmy exchanged
his old life for God's eternal life. Later, he returned to Indiana,
married, raised a family, and lived a useful life. It was said
that each evening he would gather his family together for
prayer and always there was the petition, "God bless Pacific
Garden Mission!"

The Clarkes were indeed happy together in the Lord's service
as they watched their family of spiritual children grow. But in
1892 Mother Clarke was left alone when God called the Colonel from his labors. The Mission mother's heart was saddened

but, with Harry Monroe stepping in as superintendent, she worked on. In a tribute to the memory of her husband, she wrote:

> I'm coming soon to meet you, dear,
> The journey now is almost o'er;
> A few more sheaves to gather here,
> We'll meet up there to part no more.

But it wasn't really to be soon. For nearly a quarter of a century after that, as long as her health held up, the Mission mother continued faithfully gathering in sheaves. And she was to live to see one of the sheaves she and the Colonel had already brought in (in 1886) become one of the greatest evangelists of all time.

Chapter 5

KID IN THE SAGE-GREEN SUIT

IN THE EARLY 1880's a train from Marshalltown, Iowa, eased into Chicago. Off stepped a country lad with uncut hair wearing a sage-green suit. After inquiring about directions, he legged it to A. G. Spalding's old store at 108 Madison Street. Strangely, though he arrived at 7 A.M., the store wasn't open; the lad himself had always gone to work at the 7 o'clock whistle.

Fingering the dollar he had in his pocket—all the money he had left after buying the green suit—he waited. Finally at 8:00 the store opened, and the young man showed a clerk a telegram he had gotten from Marshalltown's Pop Anson, captain of the National League's Chicago White Stockings (now the Cubs). That was his passport.

"So your name's Billy Sunday?" the clerk mused. "How'd Pop get on to you?"

"His aunt Em's a great baseball fan," Billy explained. "She always came out to see our Marshalltown team play. And she even went to Des Moines and watched us whip 'em 15 to 6 for the state championship. I did a few things in that game. Aunt Em kept telling Cap Anson to give me a try, and here I am."

About 10:00 Dalrymple, the left fielder of the Chicago club and batting champion of the National League, strolled in. Others came. Billy was introduced to them. He felt more and more like a hayseed as he compared himself to these well-groomed professional athletes.

Finally, Cap Anson came in and welcomed Billy warmly. Then with a twinkle in his eye he said, "Billy, they tell me

44

that you can run some. Fred Pfeffer is our crack runner. How about putting on a little race at the ball park this morning?"

"Anything you say, Mr. Anson," Billy squeaked.

Soon they went to the ball park on the lakefront, situated on Michigan Avenue from Randolph Street to Adams Street. Larry Cochrane, one of the pitchers, lent Billy a uniform. It didn't exactly fit. And not owning baseball shoes, Billy chose to run barefoot. So there were chuckles galore as Billy and Pfeffer got set for the race.

"Go!" Cap Anson shouted.

A moment later the players were pounding Billy on the back and good-naturedly jeering Pfeffer. The hayseed kid had won by fifteen feet!

Winning the race opened the hearts of the players to Billy Sunday and made the first step toward a regular job with the Chicago club. As he was leaving the ball park following practice, Cap asked him, "Got any money for a place to stay and eats?"

"Yeah, a dollar."

With an oath, Cap tossed him a 20 dollar gold piece.

At first Billy served as treasurer of the club, but then the day came when he stepped into the batter's box in an actual game. Recounting his early experiences, Sunday wrote:

"I struck out the first four or five times at bat. The ball would pass me and be on its way back to the pitcher before I swung at it. I corrected this defect by using a lighter bat and not gripping it clear to the end. . . . Then, I used to pull away from the ball; instead of stepping straight ahead with my right foot, I stepped away from the plate. The pitcher would keep the ball on the farther side of the plate and I'd miss the old apple. Mike Kelly showed me how to do it, and I soon caught on. One season I batted .356 and was fourteenth in the list."

Even so, Sunday was never a great hitter—adequate, to be sure, averaging about .260. But his defensive ability and blinding speed brought fans to their feet and gray hairs to the heads

of opposing managers. He was the first man to circle the bases
in 14 seconds. He stole bases with a headfirst slide and stretched
singles into two-baggers and two-baggers into triples. One opposing manager ordered his players to throw to the base ahead
of the one they would ordinarily throw to if the runner was
Billy.

But little did Sunday or anyone else dream that one day he
would become even better known in the Lord's service as a
world-renowned evangelist. In his early baseball days he was
as tough, rough, and profane as the next ball player of that day.
But a sudden change came into Sunday's life in 1886 after he
had been with the White Stockings three years. He once told
about it in these words:

"I walked down State Street in Chicago one Sunday afternoon
with some baseball players whose names were world renowned.
We entered a saloon and drank and then walked to the corner
of State and Van Buren Streets, which was then a vacant lot.
Some men and women were in a Gospel Wagon, playing instruments and singing gospel hymns that I heard my mother sing in
the log cabin out in Iowa. We sat on the curbstone and listened.
A man rose. His name was Harry Monroe, an ex-gambler and
counterfeiter.

"Well, we sat on the curb listening to men and women playing on cornets and trombones and singing gospel hymns that
many of the churches have blue-penciled as being too crude for
these so-called enlightened days. Harry Monroe stepped out and
said, 'Don't you men want to hear the story of men who used to
be dips [pickpockets], yeggs [safecrackers], burglars, second-
story men, drunkards, and have done time in the big house, and
who today are sober, honest, have good homes, and are trusted
and respected; of women who used to sell their womanhood to
whoever would buy, were slaves to dope and drink, and are now
married and have children of their own? Come down to the
Mission and hear stories of redeemed lives that will stir you no

matter whether you have even been inside of a church or have wandered away from God and decency.'

"I turned to the crowd that sat there with me and said, 'Boys, I bid the old life good-bye.' Some laughed, some smiled, some shrugged their shoulders, and some looked with mingled expressions of admiration and disgust. One fellow said, 'All right, Billy, if that's the way you feel about it.'

"I went to the Pacific Garden Mission that evening and liked what I heard. I went back again and again, and one night I went forward and publicly accepted Christ as my Saviour. If the same floor is in that old building, I can show you the knothole in the board upon which I knelt that dark and stormy night. I have followed Jesus from that day to this every second, like the hound on the trail of the fox, and will continue until He leads me through the pearly gate into the presence of God and it [the gate] closes on its jeweled hinges."

For three nights after he met Christ, Billy "never slept a wink," he told his audiences later in great evangelistic campaigns. He was afraid of "the horselaugh the boys would give" when they showed up for practice. He entered the ball park "with fear and trembling," saying to himself, *I am not a thief. I am not a drunkard. Why should I worry?*

The first man to meet him grabbed his hand. It was Mike Kelly, one of the top players in the league. He said, "Billy, I see by the papers what you have done. Religion ain't my long suit, and I haven't been to mass for so long I have forgotten how the priest looks. But I won't knock you, my boy, and if anyone does I will knock them." Then came Pop Anson and others—Clarkson, Flint, Williamson, Gore, Burns, Dalrymple—all with an encouraging word. "I felt as if a millstone had been dropped from my shoulders," Sunday remarked later.

Billy Sunday became an even better baseball player after his encounter with the Saviour. In the very first game as a new Christian he found the pressure on as the White Stockings sought to hold a 3 to 2 lead in the ninth inning. Detroit had two out, a man on second, and a man on third. Charlie Bennett, their catcher, was at bat. He had two strikes and three balls on him. John Clarkson, great White Stockings pitcher, reared back and sought to throw high and close, knowing Bennett's weakness. But his foot slipped, and the ball sailed in low and Charlie hit it on the nose.

Sunday turned at the crack of the bat and started back toward the stands in the right field. As he sought to outrun the ball, he prayed: "O Lord, I'm in an awful hole. If You ever helped me, please do it now, and You haven't much time to make up Your mind."

Seeing that the ball was about to drop into the edge of the crowd, Sunday yelled, "Get out of the way!" He leaped, and the ball hit and stuck in his glove. He tumbled to the turf but jumped up with the ball in hand. Pandemonium broke loose as excited fans threw cushions, pop bottles, and hats into the air. Tom Johnson, later mayor of Cleveland, Ohio, hugged Sunday and shoved a 10-dollar bill into his hand, saying, "Billy, buy yourself a new hat and come to the Palmer House tomorrow, and I will buy you the best suit of clothes in Chicago." Next day he bought Sunday his first tailor-made suit.

After a hilarious welcome in the clubhouse, Billy dressed and was met outside by a dark-brown-eyed, black-haired girl named Helen Thompson. She threw her arms around him and kissed him. "That was OK," Sunday observed. "We were engaged." They were married on September 5, 1888.

Sunday played five years with Chicago and then transferred to Pittsburgh for a year and then to Philadelphia. From the time of his conversion, he became an eager Bible student. As months passed he testified in local churches and invited people to come to Christ. In Philadelphia God's work loomed more important than even his beloved baseball. But to complicate matters, Sunday was offered a new contract for 3,500 dollars, a top figure of those days. He declined it. Later, he explained:

"I had a three-year contract with Philadelphia. I said to God,

'Now if You want me to quit playing ball and go into evangelistic work, then You get me my release.' And so I left it with God to get my release before the 25th day of March and would take that as an evidence that He wanted me to quit.

"On the 17th day of March—St. Patrick's Day, I shall never forget it—I received a letter from Colonel Rogers, president of the Philadelphia club, stating I could have my release."

Billy quit baseball and entered the YMCA as an assistant secretary at $83.33 per month—a far cry from the 500 dollars he would have received as a player. And sometimes his $83.33 was six months overdue, for the "Y" in those days was poor, though fervent in proclaiming the gospel. Billy had a hard time of it at first, sometimes barely having enough to pay his house rent. But this was all according to God's plan. Eventually Billy Sunday became an evangelist who led thousands of souls to Christ until his death at 72 on November 6, 1935.

In the more than 40 years he preached, he never forgot the Old Lighthouse where he responded to the glorious gospel. For many years he served on the Mission's board of trustees. In his great campaigns across the land he told of the great work of God in the mission outpost in Chicago. When in Chicago, he and "Ma" Sunday often dropped into the Mission and gave a word of testimony; and they often participated in anniversary rallies, helping raise money for the annual budget.

As a further encouragement, Sunday remembered his spiritual birthplace with financial gifts. When he closed a ten-week campaign in Chicago, he gave a cash love offering of 42,000 dollars, the net income after campaign expenses. That gift paid two-thirds of the cost of moving the Mission in January 1923 to its present address on South State Street.

But years before the Mission moved from Van Buren Street, while Sunday was still in baseball, a new era was beginning in the little soul-winning station.

Chapter 6

THE REIGN OF HARRY MONROE

WITH THE PASSING of Colonel Clarke in 1892, round-faced, thickset Harry Monroe, a man's man as well as God's man, stepped into the driver's seat at the Mission, though Mrs. Clarke remained very much in the picture as the Mission mother.

The glorious procession of transformed men continued as the excounterfeiter pressed home the claims of Christ. Harry's own story was known far and wide. Billy Sunday told it time and again in his meetings across the land, as did Mel Trotter, who came to Christ under Monroe in 1897.* And it was not unusual that some of the details of Harry's story spread through the twilight world of the levee, sending hoboes and other riffraff shuffling into the Mission one by one to get a look at the new leader of the rescue station. When they didn't come to the Mission, he took the gospel to them, having introduced the idea of the Gospel Wagon. From the horse-drawn wagon, workers preached, gave testimonies, and sang the gospel to people on the street. These outdoor services were the forerunners of the famous street meetings of later years.

Some of those who visited the Mission were small-time hoodlums who learned to respect Monroe and occasionally confided in him. If one would hint at plans for pulling a job, Harry pleaded with him not to carry out his crime but to come to Christ and begin laying up treasures in heaven.

From the standpoint of homiletics, Monroe would have flunked at the outset in a contest to name Chicago's most pol-

*See chapter 7.

ished preacher, for he was simply not a great preacher. He had little formal Bible training, yet he stuck to sound doctrine. Mainly, of course, he proclaimed that Jesus could unshackle the worst of sinners, and every message was intended to move them to the Saviour. Harry shook sinners over the fires of hell and then sought to lead them right to Calvary.

Billy Sunday and Mel Trotter were, of course, the outstanding converts of Monroe's day, but there were countless others who also turned from idols and began to worship the true and living God under his influence. Many went into some form of full-time gospel work, including Lew Speegle, Jacob Dudley, George Preston, John Troy, and Martin O'Connor.

Ed Card also came to Christ during the reign of Harry Monroe, and his life was marvelously transformed. Only in recent years have full details come to light, thanks to the patient research of Jack Odell, writer-director of PGM's radio program, "Unshackled!" Mission records had indicated that Card met Christ during the Monroe years and went on to become superintendent of the Sunshine Mission in St. Louis, Missouri. Odell discovered that Card actually had never made much of his story. When pressed for details, about all he would say was, "The old days? Well, I'll tell you. I was a great drunkard and a great sinner."

Ed was born in Nova Scotia in 1853. As a young man, he came to Chicago where he landed a job as a railway express messenger. He became a good employee in the eyes of his employer and earned a promotion to agent. It must have been about then that he married. In time there were two children. Their early impressions of their daddy, however, were spoiled by the fact that by this time Ed had become a hard drinker. As usually happens, there was a period during which he was able to juggle his drinking and his job. His wife did her best to cover up for him when he disappeared, but there was a limit to how long that could continue.

Then finally it happened. The boss came to his home and

Ed wasn't there. His wife made the announcement when Ed returned:

"You're fired, Ed. They don't want you there anymore. Your boss brought your last paycheck."

As the words sunk in, Ed muttered, "Nobody wants Ed Card. But, yes, I know somebody who wants me." He beckoned to one of his daughters. "Come here, Pettie."

The small girl backed away and cowered behind her mother's long skirt. "Mama! I'm afraid of Daddy."

Ed dejectedly stumbled out of the house to find another drink. He didn't come back—not that night nor for a good many nights. In time, as he became more and more disreputable-looking, bartenders drove him out almost as fast as the weather drove him in. And, in this condition, Ed Card hit Skid Row.

The night he stumbled into Pacific Garden Mission, Ed heard the voice of Harry Monroe preaching of the unshackling power of Jesus Christ. But his brain reeled, and he fell to the floor. Monroe called, "Somebody help that man!"

Mother Clarke helped revive him. When some of the liquor had left Ed's brain, she talked to him about placing his trust in Christ to free him from sin and all that had dragged him to the gutter. Finally he put his whole case in the hands of the almighty Saviour.

Paul wrote, "If any man be in Christ, he is a new creature" (II Cor. 5:17). Ed Card became walking evidence of the truth of that statement. Probably the first real proof occurred when Ed went back to his wife and children. They discovered that they had a *new* daddy.

Later, after helping start Sunshine Mission in St. Louis, Ed Card became superintendent, serving the mission from April 1903 till his death 30 years later on February 20, 1933. A kindly man with a white mustache and known as "Daddy" Card, he often said: "I would rather kneel beside a poor help-less man than have all the gold in St. Louis. To win a soul for Jesus Christ is for me the greatest joy I know."

Thus Card carried on in the tradition of Harry Monroe, who was preaching the night he came to Christ. Monroe himself was a master at soul-winning, both in dealing personally with individuals and pointing them to the Lamb of God and in drawing the net in meetings. It was Monroe who taught Billy Sunday his first lessons in giving the invitation and in talking man-to-man with a sinner regarding the steps of salvation.

Annually in his last years at the Mission, Harry reported to Sunday and Mel Trotter of God's continued blessings at the Old Lighthouse when the Great Triumvirate—as Carl Henry termed them in his book, *A Doorway to Heaven*—came together at a retreat for mission workers at Winona Lake, Indiana. By this time Sunday had made his home at Winona. Ma Sunday would cook a country dinner for these three great converts of the Mission, and they would talk over old times as they ate chicken, mashed potatoes, green beans, tomatoes, hot biscuits, and all the trimmings.

In the year 1912 tragedy struck, causing Mission trustees to look for a new superintendent. Monroe had labored nearly 32 years in the Old Lighthouse from the year of his conversion. He spent 20 of those years as its leader. On the verge of a nervous breakdown, probably brought on by overwork, Harry walked one night off a moving train and suffered injuries that took him away from the Mission except for occasional visits. Mel Trotter stepped in to hold things together, for Mother Clarke was now 77 and had been severely injured in an accident in a revolving door of a State Street department store.

By 1915, Monroe felt well enough to accompany Mel Trotter on a nationwide tour, but in December he became so ill that he was hospitalized. In July 1916 he died in his home in Morgan Park. Monroe was buried in Mount Greenwood Cemetery, not far from the grave of the man whom he succeeded, Colonel Clarke.

Mother Clarke lived for another two years, during which time she was a complete invalid, unable to converse with anyone. She had been nursed by Anna Andrews, who left her bedside only one day in six years. The nurse dropped dead in January 1918 and two weeks later, never recovering from the shock, Mother Clarke joined her beloved Colonel and Harry Monroe.

The Mission mother's estate, most of it resulting from Colonel Clarke's earlier business investments, came to about 100,000 dollars. She left it all to Pacific Garden Mission. This was a blessing, for active supporters of the work numbered only seventy-five. Harry Monroe had remembered the Old Lighthouse too, willing 1000 dollars to be charged against his real estate. However, it was discovered that he had not left any real estate and had little personal property. The Mission trustees therefore passed a motion waiving any claims the Mission might have against his estate. And no one was sorry at all, for it was no surprise that Harry Monroe had so few earthly treasures. He had spent well over a quarter of a century doing nothing but winning souls. The fact is, he had loved his job so much and considered it so important in a right sense that he had once said, "I'd rather be superintendent of Pacific Garden Mission than president of the United States!"

Among converts of the Mission, probably only one man surpassed Harry Monroe as a mission leader—his old friend Mel Trotter, the drink-mad hobo who came to Christ under Monroe's ministry.

Chapter 7

BAREFOOT WALK ON SUICIDE ROAD

AN ICY WIND off Lake Michigan stabbed through his thin clothes as Mel Trotter, the hobo, dropped off a boxcar in Chicago in January 1897. Uppermost in his mind was a problem: how to get money for a drink to ease his mad thirst. Despite the freezing temperature, he sold his shoes and bought a drink. Then lonely, desperate he considered his next move as in his stocking feet he stumbled along ice-covered streets hour after hour. Nobody seemed to notice him.

Trotter had been in Chicago on other occasions; he knew Skid Row only too well. This dark, twisted, devil-ridden section of town swallowed him up without a notice, and nobody cared how often he drifted in and out of town riding the rods.

To Trotter, no one aside from his wife, Lottie, seemed to care about him at all. One miserable, wet night another unpaying passenger had pushed him off a moving freight train. As he lay in the mud, bleeding and drunk, he had stopped caring.

This had been a climax to a series of blows in Trotter's existence. To begin with he had made unwise choices in his early years.

As Mel grew up in Freeport, Illinois, his dad, William Trotter, had been a bartender and an alcoholic. His mother, Emily, thoroughly believed in prayer, and she taught him a prayer when he was a child that was to dog him all his life: "Now I lay me down to sleep, I pray the Lord my soul to keep."

When Mel was 17, he became a school dropout and began

55

drifting. Finally he became a barber, but the taste for liquor he had learned from his father began to control him. First, he found himself getting skinned in poker games and then losing customers. After all, nobody wants his neck shaved by a barber with the morning-after shakes!

But Mel braced up time after time. During one of his braced-up times, he met and married a wonderful girl, Lottie. Little did she know that his first love was alcohol.

But it didn't take her long to find it out. He stumbled into the house one day, and innocent little Lottie thought he was sick! Then things added up, "Mel, you—you're drunk!" And then she said painfully, "Have you ever been like this before?"

He had to admit the truth. But instead of leaving him, or even becoming angry, Lottie whispered, "Mel, I love you, and I'll help you all I can." She didn't mention prayer that night, but Mel began to sense that she wasn't taking this blow alone. Lottie belonged to the same God to whom his mother prayed.

That was only the first shock for Lottie. Not long afterward Mel lost his barbering job because of his drinking. But Lottie was so understanding that he made her a promise, a big promise. "Lottie, I'm never gonna touch another drink as long as I live. Honest!"

Lottie was encouraged, and then she shared a secret with Mel, something to help him keep his promise: "Honey, we're going to have a baby!"

Mel walked with a firmer step and held his head higher in the days that followed. Soon he got a job as an insurance salesman, and for weeks he did well. Then gambling habits took over. He gambled to fatten his earnings so he'd have plenty for the new baby. But he lost and then gambled to make up the deficit. The vicious circle got tighter and tighter until the day after his son was born when he lost the insurance job too!

Into this black abyss flickered a ray of light, of hope, in the person of a kindly friend. Trying to cheer Mel, he said, "You've tried like I've never seen a man try to give up this drinking habit. You've tried all the cures; I know that. But I think I've got a plan that'll really do the trick for you."

Then he told Mel about a vacant farmhouse he owned, 11 miles from the nearest town and saloon. He wanted the Trotters to live there away from the temptation of liquor.

"I honestly hate liquor now," Mel responded. "I'll take you up on your offer."

The Trotters moved to the little farm. For three glorious months they were like honeymooners—with the little boy. During that time Mel didn't touch the bottle once. But what Lottie didn't know was that, for the last two months, a craving for drink was gnawing right through Mel's will power.

"You ta-take the baby inside, Honey," he told Lottie after a happy buggy ride one winter night. "I'll put the horse away, and I'll be right in."

But as the door closed, he wheeled the horse and buggy around and lashed the horse into a mad dash for town. Mel licked his lips, hardly able to wait to walk into the town saloon to order his first drink since he had moved to the farm.

After a few drinks, he was the same old wisecracking, devil-may-care Mel. "Hey, fellows, drinks are on me. The bartender can have my horse and buggy. Let's drink 'im dry!"

Next morning an alcohol-soaked Mel staggered the 11 miles home, the 11 miles that was supposed to separate him and drink forever!

Wet-eyed and unsmiling, Lottie helped him in as tenderly as ever. Just her look and touch broke Mel up, and once again he swore off drinking and promised her he'd never do this to her again.

With the horse and buggy guzzled away in that one lost night, Mel, Lottie, and the boy had to move back to the city. Mel could hardly farm without a horse, and there was no money for another one. The new place was hardly a home—just a cold, bare room off a hallway.

One day Mel came back to the room, cursing himself for

having made himself out a wretched liar once again, this time by a ten-day drunk. As he opened the door, he paled. Lottie was just placing their son on the old iron bed, and he immediately knew something was wrong. Then he heard Lottie pray: "Father, God, I've had my thoughts on my baby more than on You. Now, I want to turn to You. You are all I have left."

The little son was dead!

Mel rushed outdoors in a frenzy and hardly knew what he was doing until he returned home the next afternoon. Lottie was still there, this time with a little white casket. She thought this bitter blow would bring Mel to his senses. "Mel, Honey, surely now you'll give up drink for good."

Red-eyed, Mel choked out, "I promise."

Two hours after his son's funeral he came home again—blind drunk! Lottie turned as if she were leaving, but instead she dropped to her knees and prayed with her hand holding Mel's: "Lord, I'm Your child. From this day I'm going to serve only You and others. You have my baby with you now. I still have my husband, and I love him very much. By Your grace I shall pray that he will someday belong to You as I do. And I believe he will."

Lottie's faith that Mel would find God never wavered. Perhaps she had been praying for him that night when he had been shoved from the moving freight, for as he lay in the mud that little prayer his mother taught him seeped through his brain and lips, "Now I lay me down to sleep, I pray the Lord my soul to keep."

Perhaps she was praying for him as he wandered Chicago's Skid Row that cold January day in 1897. His feet were beyond feeling as he hobbled along Chicago's icy streets. Tears trickled from his eyes, partly because of the cold, partly because of the voice that kept taunting him. "Trotter, you're hopeless. You're a no-good bum. The world would be better off without you. Keep walking east. Let the murky waters of Lake Michigan get you out of your misery."

Stumbling along on Van Buren toward the lake, another drink guzzled to give him courage, Mel turned wildly as a curly haired man seized his arm. With a cheerful word, he led him through a door into a warm building and propped him up on two wooden chairs. For a time Mel didn't know he was in the Pacific Garden Mission, nor that his sympathetic escort was Tom Mackay, an ex-drunkard and cardsharp who had been converted from his misery and sin to Christ only a few weeks earlier.

Mel stirred and glanced toward the front of the room where a man was praying. "O God, we ask You right now, move in that poor boy's heart and mind and save him!" Somehow Mel knew that the man was praying for him.

He fell asleep; and when he awoke, he heard that same voice, the voice of Mission Superintendent Harry Monroe, telling about his conversion from counterfeiting. One sentence in particular struck Mel: "I was just 27 years old when I happened into the Pacific Garden Mission—just 27 years old."

Mel was just 27 years old too, and it began to dawn on him that he was in a mission—not in Lake Michigan.

Harry Monroe kept talking, and a warmth crept into Mel's heart. Though he never quite knew what turned the tide in his heart, he was soon staggering down the aisle, hoping someone could do something for him. He cried out to God that night for forgiveness, and God heard his sincere cry—for a sense of forgiveness flooded his soul.

From that night the thirst for alcohol left him, and God gave him complete victory. He learned that Jesus had said, "If any man thirst, let him come unto me, and drink" (John 7:37). Mel did that, and Jesus took away the other evil thirst. Lottie's prayers were answered!

The Pacific Garden Mission became the brightest spot in Chicago to Mel Trotter. It was natural for him to go into the same kind of work. In order to rescue other lost souls like his had been, he helped to found sixty other rescue missions around the country. Billy Sunday often called on Mel, at the conclusion of the great Sunday campaigns, to "come and help the brethren" get started with a rescue mission. From 1912 to 1918 Trotter served as general superintendent or overseer of Pacific Garden Mission, though he necessarily had to spend most of his time at the thriving mission he founded in Grand Rapids, Michigan. During this period the Chicago mission was actively led by able acting superintendents, including Bob Ingersoll, who served from 1916 to 1918.

As the years went by and Trotter preached the gospel across the country, people got to calling him the happiest man in the world and "the man who raves about Jesus." When the theologians wanted to ordain him into the ministry, they tossed up some pretty tough questions for a boy who didn't even finish high school. But the clincher was a breeze that even a doctor of theology couldn't trip him up on:

"How do you know you were made a new man in Christ?"

Mel wasn't joking when he replied: "Gentlemen, that's easy. I was there when it happened!"

On his spiritual birthday anniversary, Mel always arranged a great testimony meeting at his Grand Rapids mission. His own testimony was always the highlight of the program. In January 1940 it appeared that he would be too ill to observe his forty-third spiritual anniversary in the customary manner. He had become ill on a tour to the British Isles and had been hospitalized. But he asked God for a bit of extra strength and came to the meeting, speaking a few words to the large audience. It was his last public appearance at his mission.

On September 11, 1940, Mel Trotter died at the age of 72 at his home in Macatawa Park, near Grand Rapids. Today thousands still remember Mel as their spiritual father and others thank God for him and the sixty rescue stations God used him to plant in cities across America. At Pacific Garden Mission he will never be forgotten. Not only is he one of the greatest converts of the Old Lighthouse but when the going was rugged in the years of World War I, Mel kept the light burning brightly until God brought another husband-wife team on the scene as keepers.

Chapter 8

PA AND MA TO SKID ROW

THE STORY Charles E. Crawford was telling especially impressed the Mission pianist, Ma Taylor, that night back in the 1920's. Crawford, who worked at the American Bible Society, was giving his testimony in a Mission meeting:

"My heart sank the time I was told by my district manager that I would have to be bonded. For I knew that in the light of my record before conversion, no bonding company would accept the risk." Heartbroken, Crawford had stolen away to the shipping room to pray. Then, his face beaming, he testified that later the district manager got a report from the Bible Society's governing board. "They voted to waive the rule and I didn't have to be bonded. In spite of the fact that my record was black as midnight before I came to Christ, the board recognized that Calvary covers it all," he boomed out to the Mission audience. "I not only was to continue my work without being bonded but my salary was increased!"

Out of his testimony that night came these words from the pen of Ma Taylor:

Calvary covers it all,
My past with its sin and stain.
My guilt and despair,
Jesus took on Him there,
And Calvary covers it all.

Within a short time Ma Taylor had completed "Calvary Covers It All," and it quickly became a song sung across America and around the world. Almost sixty gospel songs flowed from the pen of Ma Taylor, but none better summarizes the message she and Pa Taylor proclaimed the eighteen years they served at the Mission than "Calvary Covers It All."

The Taylors were keepers of the Old Lighthouse from 1918, through the Roaring Twenties, and on till 1936. Pa's foghorn voice stopped many a derelict dead in his tracks and turned him into the open door of the Mission. As Pa preached the gospel and told how to find forgiveness of sin through Christ, Ma prayed for the outcasts of society who filled the Mission. And then as the invitation was given, she was at the piano playing and praying that the prayer room would be filled. Quite often it was.

It was Pa Taylor's preaching and Ma Taylor's praying that God used to transform Walter "Happy Mac" MacDonald, who went on to become a famous evangelist, preaching across America and Canada for nearly thirty years until his death in 1963. He came to Christ under most unusual circumstances. A vaudeville comedian, MacDonald was finding it harder and harder to keep his audiences laughing as whiskey threatened his very career. Accepting the invitation of Miss Alberta Schultz, a new Christian, to attend a service at Pacific Garden Mission, MacDonald was captivated by what he heard. When he wasn't busy with an engagement as entertainer, he dropped into Mission meetings for more of the powerful preaching of Walter Taylor, the rousing singing, and the testimonies.

One night the comedian, so much under the influence of alcohol that his body trembled, sat listening once again to a forceful message. MacDonald sobered noticeably as the preacher's crooked index finger seemed to point again and again at him. Then words that Taylor quoted from Psalm 2 completely unnerved the vaudeville funny man: "He that sitteth in the heavens shall laugh" (Ps. 2:4). Then followed a penetrating laugh from the preacher as he interpreted how God's laughter might sound.

This haunted MacDonald until he returned to the Mission the

next night, May 29, 1925, failing for the first time to fill his engagement as an entertainer. At the moment he was scheduled to be entertaining, he was instead on his knees confessing to God his sin and need of the Saviour.

Turning his back on the entertainment field, MacDonald assisted the Taylors in their work at the Mission for two years, singing and leading song services. As he grew in grace and knowledge of Christ, he came to love his spiritual parents in a greater way. At times it seemed that Walter Taylor, an able preacher who knew the Bible well, was too hard on him as he sought to ground the new convert in the Word. "You're not worth your salt unless you read the Bible and pray," the superintendent told him. But such training paid off, and MacDonald often thanked God for the schooling he got under the Taylors. It was he who first called them "Ma" and "Pa."

MacDonald not only got excellent tutoring from Pa Taylor in preaching and introducing individuals to Christ but around the Mission he put the teaching to work in practical experience. On one occasion he dealt with one of his old drinking buddies, Doc, the gravel-voiced barker for a burlesque house on South State. Reconstructed, the story unfolded in this way:

"Well, if it ain't the little Reverend Happy Mac," Doc greeted sardonically one day as MacDonald was walking down the street. "Happy, say it's a lie! Say it ain't true that them Mission heads got my old pal."

"No, Doc, it isn't a lie. I've become a Christian. I'm through with the old life."

Things climaxed later when eight of his old drinking friends, including Doc, met MacDonald on the street. They lined up, four on each side, and he had to walk between. MacDonald spoke, and they responded with, "One, two, three—*ptoo!*" They spit on his new tan suit and shoes. Unlike the Happy of old, he responded pleasantly, "Your aim is excellent, Doc. Caught my new trouser leg and my shoe."

"That all you got to say?" Doc glared.

"Not quite, Doc. There's this: When you get to know Jesus Christ the way I've just this minute discovered I know Him, you'll be able to unclench your fists. You'll let a guy spit on you, and it'll be all right!"

MacDonald didn't see Doc again for three weeks. One night from the Mission platform he noticed him sitting in the audience on the front row! As the invitation was given that evening, Happy Mac hopped down from the platform and slipped into a seat beside Doc.

"Doc, what did you come for tonight?"

"You're not mad at me, Happy?"

"The Lord won't let me get mad anymore, Doc."

"Happy, you been a Christian long enough to know how to lead a guy to Jesus?"

"Yes, Doc." Joy surged in MacDonald's heart.

"Then I'm your customer."

Old Doc showed MacDonald a letter that had resulted in his coming to the Mission. His aged mother was dying, and he was about to go to her bedside. And to prepare, he had first to become a Christian. "I promised my mother I'd do it before she died. She's waited 54 years for me to do it. But now that you've led me to Jesus, I'm gonna beat it home," Doc revealed. "Pray, Happy, that I'll get there in time to tell her all about it."

Two weeks later Doc was back in Chicago. He'd had three hours with his mother, and his news had brought great joy to her heart.

Doc continued on the street—but now helping the Taylors as MacDonald had been doing. His job was to invite people to come into the Old Lighthouse to find Christ. But one day a couple of weeks after he started, Doc dropped dead on the sidewalk. He joined his old mother with the Saviour.

Pa and Ma Taylor had been handpicked for the job of keepers of the Lighthouse by Mel Trotter—and God. Great things had been happening at the Mission, and Trotter, anxious to devote full time to his Grand Rapids mission, wired the Taylors. Their background made them a perfect team.

Pa Taylor had, in the years when the Clarkes were nursing the Mission along in its infancy, been successful in business. Then a year before Mel Trotter was converted, Walter Grand Taylor, 30, grief-stricken over the death of his first wife, came to Christ in his room. The date was February 21, 1896. His wife had been a Christian, and he also wanted to be ready to meet God.

Spiritually alive and full of zeal, Taylor left the business world and went into YMCA work. Soon he enrolled in Moody Bible Institute where practical work assignments took him to Pacific Garden Mission. Here he met Mel Trotter, Harry Monroe, Mother Clarke, and others. His first convert was U. S. Abell, later a widely known Christian cartoonist, who came to the Mission in 1897.

Wedding bells sounded for Walter Taylor in 1898 as Dr. R. A. Torrey officiated. His bride was Ethelwyn "Bobbie" Robinson, whom he met in a Christian boarding house when she volunteered to play the piano while he sang a solo.

The newlyweds began praying that God would direct them into His chosen work for them. After Walter graduated from Moody Bible Institute in 1900, they served briefly in the Parkhurst Church House, New York, and then went to Colorado for a year as home missionaries among railroad men and miners. Here he began feeling like a runaway Jonah, for God had been speaking to him about doing mission work. He shuddered as he remembered an incident when he had been assisting in services at Pacific Garden Mission:

A dapper dresser, with wavy, golden hair, Taylor compassionately put his arm around the shoulders of down-and-outers while praying with them. Once Mel Trotter came up and quietly lifted Taylor's arm away. Walter didn't think much about it at the time. But one night, after the meeting, he mentioned to Mel that he had a problem:

"Tell me, Mel, do you ever find yourself itching at the end

of a meeting? I feel as though something were crawling around inside my shirt and biting me."

Trotter smiled and straightened out young Taylor quickly: "Now you know why I keep lifting your arm off these fellows' shoulders. Lice."

Nevertheless, Taylor said yes to God concerning mission work, and he accepted a call to become superintendent of the Old Brewery Mission in Montreal. Here he grew a moustache and spent 16 years in a fruitful ministry, winning people from all walks of life—up-and-outers as well as the downtrodden, and women and children in a summer fresh air camp.

In 1918 the wire came from Mel Trotter while the Taylors were in a soul-winning ministry at Camp Sheridan; the Lighthouse in Chicago needed a keeper. Walter arrived September 3, 1918, and Mrs. Taylor came 12 days later.

A colorful character who later thanked God for the open door of the Old Lighthouse during the Taylor era was George Delos Snow—pool player, poker player, card shark, and professional cheater extraordinary. Good-looking and a great actor, he worked for the house and could deal cards from the bottom and make it appear they came from the top of the deck. He always had an ace in the hole—until the night of February 11, 1919, when he got so fed up with his rotten life that he came to the Mission. Under the ministry of T. B. Davis, who was preaching that night, he came to Christ and exchanged his old life for a new one as white as his name.

For many years he testified in churches, missions, and in the noonday meeting conducted by the Old Lighthouse at State and Harrison. In his characteristic way, he'd begin his testimony, "Well, here stands five feet five inches of Snow." Then he would go on:

"I tell you the devil had me tight, and I wasn't trying to get away either. Say, you've heard these wise guys get up and tell folks how to get rid of their bad habits. All you got to do is to sign a pledge, or join something or other, or just exert your will

power, and you can get by all right. They make me sick! Fat
chance a fellow has of exerting will power when the devil has
got him hog-tied. But you see I had something in my favor. I
had a mother who never let up praying for her boy. You'd
think she'da got discouraged and quit, for her prayers didn't
seem to be answered. But she didn't.

"Mr. Devil told me it was too late for me to change, even if
I wanted to. He'd bring to mind all the miserable, wasted years
of my past life. But, oh boy, I heard something different when
I got to the Mission. I heard of a Jesus Christ who saves men
from their sins, cleans 'em up and starts 'em all over again.
Gives them a new life and peace instead of a heartache. And,
friends, I tried it—or rather I tried Him—and it worked! I went
to see my mother right away afterwards. When I met her I said,
'Ma, I went down to Pacific Garden Mission last night and got
saved.' And she said, 'Oh, thank God! I can die happy now.'
And later she did too, and she's up there now waiting for me."

Another trophy of grace during the Taylor years was Scotty
Lawrence. This songwriter was so talented he once took a bet
that in twenty minutes he could write a song that would become
a national hit, and he proceeded to do it in half the time. Drink
and dope dragged him down to Skid Row, but one night in 1921
he opened his heart to Christ as Ma Taylor and two other
women knelt beside him and prayed him into the Kingdom.

Cleaned up both on the inside and outside, Scotty went to
New York, later married, and spent years in children's work
and writing glad gospel songs. The first stanza of his very first
song summarized his testimony:

> One day in sin I was told of a love
> Coming from One who is reigning above,
> Gladly I listened, 'twas music to me,
> To know, tho' a sinner, that I could be free.

It was during the Taylor years, in 1922, that a trustee Louis
A. Crittenton sat successively with an adding machine on two

Chicago street corners, counting pedestrians passing the Mission at 67 West Van Buren and those passing State and Polk Streets. His tabulation bore out what many had believed all along— fishing was better on State Street than on Van Buren, for the hobo jungle was shifting. Actually the tape revealed the fishing should be 17 times better on State Street than on Van Buren.

State Street had been dubbed "Murderer's Row" because of the number of people killed there year after year. For many blocks south of the el tracks Satan peddled his wares in the most brazen manner. Along the Row some 5000 men flopped nightly in the cheap hotels. The Mission trustees believed God was leading them into this stronghold of Satan, and the most promising building was at 650 South State. Formerly it had housed the notorious White House, a den of drink and sex. The trustees voted to buy the building and later paid 67,000 dollars for it—42,000 dollars from Billy Sunday's Chicago campaign offering and the balance from Mother Clarke's estate.

The first meeting at this site was held on Wednesday, January 31, 1923. And it was here that Pa and Ma Taylor served for 13 more years. The Taylors retired to Florida, where Pa died on October 23, 1947, and where Ma died January 20, 1951. T. Donald Gately succeeded Pa Taylor and headed the work for four years.

During this time God was preparing a young electrical me-chanic to take over in 1940 and to begin turning up the wattage of the Old Lighthouse to cause it to shine in dark places around the world as never before.

Chapter 9

GOD'S ELECTRICIAN

HARRY GEORGE SAULNIER has been associated with the Mission for a longer period than anyone else except Mother Clarke. In April 1965 the Mission staff surprised him with a testimonial party honoring him for 25 years of service as superintendent. He officially took over as keeper of the Old Lighthouse on March 1, 1940. For ten years prior to that he had assisted in services, and for six years he had served on the board of trustees.

Perhaps it was because Saulnier served on the board that he was almost overlooked as a candidate for the position of superintendent, though he and another trustee, Caspar Henning, had once tried to start a rescue mission on Chicago's North Side. Upon the resignation of Donald Gately, the board of godly businessmen overseeing the operation of the ministry thought long and hard concerning whom they could get as Lighthouse keeper. They compiled a list of 40 men, but Saulnier's name did not appear. Though the board prayed much that God would lead them in choosing a successor, weeks passed without agreement.

Finally, with Gately scheduled to leave at the end of February, the board felt that a decision definitely had to be made at their February meeting. How would God make His will known? Unable to attend the meeting, attorney Paul Fischer sent a short list of suggestions in order of preference. At the top of his list stood the name of fellow-board-member Harry Saulnier. All eyes turned on Harry as the list was read, and he sat there stunned. Until now his name had not even been whispered as a possible suggestion. Quickly, the board made a unanimous decision and gave Saulnier a week's time to make his decision.

Harry discussed the new turn of events with his wife, Gene, that night, and for a week they prayed about it. It would take a definite step of faith for him to leave the security of a good-paying job he had held for 18 years as electrical mechanic at Commonwealth Edison Company, the firm supplying power for Chicagoland. And the prospects of taking over the great responsibility of running the famous old rescue mission made the decision even more complicated. Somehow God would have to speak.

On Friday night, with time running out, Harry and Gene arose from their knees after a period of prayer. "Harry, I think the Lord wants you to say yes," Gene volunteered.

"Gene, I feel that way too," he responded thoughtfully.

Moments later Cap Henning, Harry's long-time friend and board secretary, answered his phone. "OK, Cap, I'm coming," Harry said joyfully.

At Commonwealth Edison, officials, hearing Saulnier's story, suggested that he take a six months' leave of absence and decide then if he definitely wanted to leave the company. Thus, six months later in his small office in the rear of the Mission Saulnier got a call from the Edison Company: "Six months are up. Ready to come back?" The going was by no means easy by this time, but nevertheless Harry Saulnier was having the time of his life making the light shine brighter at the Old Lighthouse. So he said a grateful "No thanks," hung up the phone, and rolled his sleeves higher. Nevertheless, just in case he should change his mind, the Edison Company extended the leave for three more months. But Harry was never to return.

In those days, as well as now, there was plenty of work to do. Somehow it seemed the ministry was resting on its laurels and not moving ahead.

In the early months, God gave Saulnier specific ideas for growth and outreach, but he realized he would have to work gradually. Humanly speaking, he couldn't immediately make drastic changes; for when he first came there was only $1.56 in the bank, and the Mission had few faithful supporters. But in those early days Saulnier began to win friends as well as souls, and he personally began to make the Mission a more efficient operation and a more inviting place for the men of the street.

Every individual has his own tastes, and a soul-winning electrician would be expected to differ in approach from his predecessors, regardless of their success. One of Saulnier's first moves was to redecorate the red, white, and blue when he arrived in March 1940. Though the blue ceiling stood for heaven, the red portion of the walls for the blood of Christ, and the white portion of the walls for the righteousness of God in Christ Jesus, the combination failed to impress Saulnier. Not that he didn't believe in the symbolism, but Skid Row men could hardly be reached through such subtle means. So, an inviting, easy-on-the-eyes beige went onto the walls and the ceiling. Except for the neatly lettered Bible texts, the men would get the gospel from the pulpit not the walls.

Next Saulnier, electrician that he was, prayed that God would help him improve the lighting system. One day he got a call from his old firm, Commonwealth Edison. They were replacing fixtures in the downtown office. Could he use some? So it was that he was up on a ladder one Saturday praying as he worked, "Lord, You've just got to help me. Send somebody, please."

About noon Arthur Burnett, of Waukegan, Illinois, walked in and looked up. "Whatcha doin'? Puttin' up new fixtures?"

"Sure. You don't happen to be an electrician, do you?"

"Yep, I just happen to be—need some help?"

Harry climbed down from the ladder, washed up, and took his newfound helper to lunch. Then they returned, and soon the Mission auditorium shone with new light.

As the months passed, Harry Saulnier desperately yearned and prayed for more space for the Mission, then housed in a single three-story building, 25′×100′. To take it out of its hole-in-the-wall category, adjoining buildings would have to be added. Most desirable of the next door buildings was the four-story Loyal Hotel, a run-down flophouse. But for years the owners only laughed at the Mission efforts to buy the hotel. They indicated that if they ever sold the property, it would be for a parking lot.

Finally, in the early months of 1941, the two buildings to the north became available, and the Mission offered 30,000 dollars. "Yet," declares Saulnier today, "we didn't have 30 cents, much less 30,000 dollars. But God began to work and by November the buildings were ours. God met our needs through gifts and a sizable loan from Christian friends."

These buildings were used for the Servicemen's Center and Women's Division, new ministries launched in Saulnier's early years.

But the matter of acquiring the Loyal Hotel continued as a burden on the hearts of the superintendent and the trustees. This added space would allow the Mission to house many more Skid Row men and thereby increase the soul-winning efficiency.

In 1955, after many contacts back and forth, the Mission got a yes from the hotel owners, provided a price tag of approximately 180,000 dollars would be agreeable. On July 7, 1955, earnest money was put down, and by November 7, 120 days later, the entire amount had been paid. God had answered fervent prayer through both small and substantial gifts. One of the miracle gifts was from a woman in Arizona who wrote and asked if the need still existed. A special delivery letter to the woman from Saulnier resulted in a 1000-dollar gift, coming a week before the final payment was due.

A few days after the signing of the final papers a crew of Mission workers, with Saulnier leading the way, moved into the old flophouse to begin the huge conversion task. Vermin-infested little cubicles, with chicken wire stretched over the tops, were torn down. Here men had flopped for 75 cents a night, the fee actually being more per cubic foot for a "room" than for most rooms at the Hilton, two blocks away on Michigan Avenue. On the first floor, the remains of a smelly, cheap tavern had to be torn out. All in all, tons of rubbish, including a rusty .32 caliber revolver found in a wall which had no doubt figured in many crimes, were carted from the old hotel during renovation.

And here, over a period of four years, God faithfully supplied funds—some 450,000 dollars—for remodeling and transforming the old building into a functional Mission unit. Today the Mission chapel occupies the tavern and hotel lobby area. The chapel is quite unlike the traditional rescue mission auditorium, being bright and cheerful, and with some 300 comfortable, modern contour chairs. The platform is attractively bordered with potted artificial flowers that are changed with the seasons: for example, spring would feature forsythia with its yellow, bell-like blossoms, and pink snapdragons. Neatly lettered Scripture texts in yellow letters on a brown background proclaim the message of salvation on the dark beige walls of the softly lighted chapel. A Hammond organ and two Baldwin pianos, one of them donated by Billy Sunday, are near the platform. The auditorium could be a church sanctuary except for the bullpen at the rear, a segregated area where drunks and others who would likely disturb a service are seated. Keeping watch over these men, who often sleep through services, are pictures of some of the heroes of faith in PGM annals—the Clarkes, Billy Sunday, Mel Trotter, Harry Monroe, and Pa Taylor.

Upstairs, where men once flopped on filthy cots, are three dormitories for Skid Row men, each identical with 75 sturdy armytype beds and toilet facilities, including 12 white porcelain showers for each floor. On the fourth floor are beds for some of the staff.

Except for new men, derelicts who look to the Mission for aid know the rules. For example, men who want lunch must arrive in time for the noon gospel service, and those who want overnight lodging must come to the evening service at 8:00.

In an increasing way under Harry Saulnier the procedure in handling men has been orderly and smooth. Except for regulations governing the flow of from 150 to 200 men at a time, utter chaos would result. After the evening service men are given tickets indicating the floor where they will sleep. Each man is frisked by a worker in order that all weapons and bottles of alcoholic beverages may be separated from their owners. In the dormitory each man checks in with his Social Security card and is given a clothes hanger with a number. He strips and hangs his clothing on the hanger, which is hung for the night in a delousing unit. Next the man showers and is given a nightshirt. His number tag directs him to the bed he is to occupy.

Next morning at 5:30 the men are awakened. The early hour is primarily for those who must report for jobs in the slave market. Those needing clothing visit the clothing room and are given clothing donated to the Mission by Christian friends. Breakfast is served at 6:30.

Through the years Saulnier has insisted on wholesome food for those served by the Mission, and today Gus Hollis and his crew of fifteen men meet those demands. The meals aren't lavish, but the food is appetizing and nourishing, plenty to hold body and soul together.

During the course of a day the kitchen crew prepares 30 gallons of cereal, 60 gallons of soup, and 30 gallons of coffee, in addition to more substantial meals for the rehabilitation staff.

Interestingly, the kitchen and dining hall, where 375 men can be served at one time, is kept spotlessly clean. After the Skid Row men vacate the area, the staff moves in. To avoid the confusion of men stumbling over chairs, Skid Row men stand to eat. Chairs are moved in for the staff and guests of the Women's and Children's Division. On Saturday nights visitors, sometimes as many as 100, are served dinner in the dining hall.

Thanksgiving, Christmas, and New Year's Day are days when

the kitchen crew serves up the biggest meals for Skid Row men. In some years as many as 800 men have been fed on these holidays. Annually, for Thanksgiving and Christmas, a poultry farm contributes a total of 2400 pounds of turkeys, and the meals served would rival those on most American tables.

During the year a number of other firms help keep the mission larder filled, cutting down considerably on expense for food. Occasionally leftover food is sent from a North Side hospital. Bread, sweet rolls, and hard rolls are regularly picked up from two bakeries and chain food stores. Large quantities of canned soups come with the compliments of a soup company.

Christians outside the Chicago area also help the Mission feed Skid Row men and women, as well as the families who come to the Old Lighthouse for aid. For example, C. W. Aeppler, of Oconomowoc, Wisconsin, who for many years was in the honey business, has since 1954 sent as many as 300 pounds of honey a month. He even furnishes honey dispensers with his own label etched on the glass in two colors with a Scripture verse included.

Big, burly Carl Dreesman, a tractor dealer from Iowa, regularly sends certain food supplies to the Mission. Saved from a life of sin and drink through the witness of Paul Hutchens (widely known writer of Christian fiction books), Dreesman made his first contribution to the Mission through Hutchens when he heard the author was coming to PGM to speak. Dreesman became so impressed with the ministry of the Mission to alcoholics and others that he then began to send the food supplies to the Mission. He also started a program among farmers in the area to collect good, usable men's, women's, and children's clothing. These he boxed and shipped regularly to the Mission through the efforts of another Christian, Cornelius Pals, a trucker, who for many years arranged and paid for each shipment. Today Dreesman, who flies his own plane, is a regular visitor, coming in for Christian fellowship at a place he learned to love before he actually saw it.

In the early days when he began to turn up the wattage of

the Old Lighthouse, Harry Saulnier had only a couple of assistants. Over the years God has sent both full-time and volunteer workers. Today the Mission has a full-time staff of some 80 men and women. Many of these regularly burn the midnight oil to get their jobs done.

The clean-up crew, under Bob Vehue, is the second largest rank-and-file unit, numbering approximately 6 to 10 men at any given time. All are men who have made professions of faith in Christ and who are being rehabilitated as they work and study the Word while living for a time at the Mission.

There are countless volunteer workers, some of whom come to the Mission regularly several times a week to assist in personal work or help with some other phase of the work.

Since 1936 teams from some 25 Chicagoland churches have conducted gospel meetings each evening in the Mission, a ministry which not only is important in the program of the Old Lighthouse but also gives men and women practical and rewarding experience in soul-winning. Most are laymen ministering the gospel through song, testimony, and preaching, as well as in man-to-man counseling in the prayer room. They are people like lanky Cliff Clark, of suburban Wheaton, who on a volunteer basis directs the work of organizing rescue mission teams at Wheaton Bible Church. A retired Pennsylvania Railroad employee, Clark makes no claim of being a preacher—but he has learned to plead earnestly for souls and to handle the Word effectively. Equally important, he shows a burden for the souls of Skid Row men. I've seen him stand up straight and tall, his shoulders back and his head up, as in prayer meeting at the church he has asked prayer for the Skid Row ministry conducted by him and his men.

Even though a different church group is in charge from evening to evening, Harry Saulnier usually appears to give the audience a friendly greeting and announcements, and often he conducts the invitation. Over the years thousands have responded to his earnest, clear-cut invitation to come to the Saviour.

Often he leaves the platform and moves among the audience speaking and pleading with men, sometimes going to the rear of the chapel to invite a man to the prayer room.

Believing there is a right and wrong way for visiting groups to deal with soul-winning activities in the Mission, Saulnier personally outlined a plan that is posted and brought to the attention of teams:

1. Group and friends meet in the prayer room at 7:30 P.M. for prayer.

2. Personal workers must kneel down with open Bible. Don't do personal work without a Bible.

3. Afterwards, bring man or woman to the person in charge of prayer room.

For the person in charge of the prayer room, rules state:

1. See that there are plenty of Gospels of John and inquiry cards.

2. Line chairs in twos.

3. See that everyone kneels when dealing with an individual —with an open Bible.

4. Question converts after they have been dealt with.

5. Be sure they have the assurance of salvation.

6. Give them a Gospel of John and have them sign on page 6.

7. Get complete information including permanent address of parent or other relatives (for follow-up).

8. Invite them to our Bible class.

One of the most important and fruitful phases of the many faceted Mission program today is the follow-up program worked out by Saulnier. As men who have made professions move on, letters go out to encourage them. Attempts are made to put them in touch with a Bible-preaching church. In addition, efforts are made to enroll all new converts in the six-lesson course on the Gospel of John, a series that has brought assurance of salvation to hundreds and caused others to place their trust in Jesus Christ for the first time. Thousands have signed up and have taken the course as a result of reading about it in the Mission's monthly paper, the *Pacific Garden Mission News*.

Under Saulnier, the anniversary rally, held usually in November though the anniversary date is September 15, has become a significant event on the evangelical calendar in Chicagoland. Some 2,000 persons generally come to the rally, held the past 18 years in the Conrad Hilton Hotel, two blocks away from the Mission on Michigan Avenue, compliments of the hotel management. Until her death in 1957, Ma Sunday, Billy's widow, was a colorful participant. Many souls are saved each year and Christians go home fired up to serve the Lord more earnestly as they hear testimonies of transformed Skid Row drifters and others.

Thus, the influence of Harry Saulnier, under the direction of the Holy Spirit, has made a world of difference in the operation and outreach of the Old Lighthouse on South State Street. Today the entire ministry is a model of efficiency, reaching the heart by means of ministering to physical needs. Saulnier takes no credit himself. He puts it this way in utmost seriousness: "Why, it's *all* a miracle of God. Even the very doorknobs are of Him!"

Chapter 10

SAULNIER, THE MAN

TOWERING FOUR STORIES above the sidewalk on the Loyal Hotel wing of the Mission, the imposing 35-foot Pa Taylor memorial sign silently proclaims to passers-by and others for several blocks to the north, south, and east: "CHRIST DIED FOR OUR SINS" and "JESUS SAVES." This sign also identifies the Mission. Cost of upkeep alone is about 78 dollars a month: 48 dollars for maintenance and about 30 dollars for electricity. A man and his mother years ago convenanted to keep the sign burning. By night especially, with its red neon letters, the sign attracts the eye. People have come to the Mission from nearby hotels after seeing the sign. Soon after the sign was erected in late 1947, the message, "JESUS SAVES," stopped an ex-newspaper reporter from suicide and he came into the Mission and found hope in Jesus Christ.

In a remarkable way the Pa Taylor sign, a visible symbol of the new Pacific Garden Mission, typifies the man whose idea it was to raise the 3500 dollars necessary to erect it. Harry Saulnier, whose second-floor office is almost within reach of the sign, stands 6 feet 3 inches, and day and night is given 100 percent to beaming forth "the glorious gospel," as he often terms it. Not only is he burdened for the souls of the unredeemed who come to the Mission and others touched through the many facets of the Old Lighthouse ministry but wherever he goes he spreads the good news by handing out gospel calendars and tracts. "No Christian is well dressed unless he has gospel tracts with him," Saulnier says. Often, under the guidance of the Holy Spirit, he will graciously explain the way of salvation to someone—on a train or plane, in a restaurant, or on the street. The place makes no difference.

On many occasions I have walked with Harry to the Dearborn Street Station, two blocks from the Mission, for dinner in the Fred Harvey Restaurant. On the way there and back it's difficult to carry on a conversation with him, for suddenly he has dropped back or turned aside. "Here's good news," I've heard him say time and again or, "A calendar for your wallet, sir!" Always, there's a friendly, warm ring to his voice and a smile to go with each piece of literature. His manly, neat appearance and the touch of white-haired dignity about him undoubtedly are used of the Spirit in these contacts.

The witnessing experiences of Harry Saulnier would fill a book. But the following serve to illustrate the fact that he is "incessantly at it," as one former, close associate put it:

Larry Foss, who was employed at the Mission for a time, says he got his baptism in tract distribution work in a Chicago train station. He was accompanying Saulnier on a deputation trip, and they arrived at the station 15 minutes early. (Hearing this, Harry's daughter Nancy exclaimed, "How could that be!") With crowds swarming on all sides, Harry took off his hat, and Larry removed his as Saulnier offered a word of prayer aloud, asking God to bless and use the tracts he held in his hand. Then Harry proceeded to divide a stack of tracts with Larry and directed Larry to begin passing them out in one area of the station while he distributed them elsewhere.

On deputation tour in Alberta, Canada, Saulnier took time out to go for a ride up a ski lift at Banff. On his way up he handed out tracts to people coming down on the ski lift a long reach away. Later, when he got to the bottom, he noticed a man reading one of the tracts, and again, typically, Saulnier, in his big, friendly way, hurried to him and said, "Hey, what do you think of it?" This opened the door for a time of man-to-man witnessing.

There have been times when Saulnier has run into trouble

with his holy boldness. On the way to Saudi Arabia by plane from Egypt, he passed out tracts as naturally as he had always done back in the U.S. At the Jedda airport he was suddenly grabbed by a couple of Muslim customs agents, and for a time "I thought I was on my way to being hanged," he chuckles. He was released, but they confiscated all his literature. Once on a train in Canada, he had given tracts to everyone in one coach and was starting on another coach. The conductor, of another religion, ordered him to stop. But Saulnier rejoiced that he had gotten as far as he did.

Visible fruit resulted from a train ride through Pennsylvania —and in this case it was the conductor himself, though Saulnier wasn't aware of it until a month later. He tells the story in these words:

"While on my way to Baltimore to speak at a mission anniversary meeting, I was passing out tracts and speaking to people here and there on the train, which was about 17 cars long. I left my open Bible on a table by my seat, with a copy of the tract 'God's Way of Salvation' nearby. At Altoona a new Pullman conductor got on. Passing through my car, he noticed the green and white cover of the tract, and he picked it up.

"I had no contact with him on the train, but a month later he came to the Mission and attended a testimony meeting I led. Dressed in his conductor's uniform he stood and gave his testimony. He said he picked up a tract, 'God's Way of Salvation,' on his train a month ago, and it brought conviction to his heart. 'Before I got to the end of my run I had read the booklet through five times,' he said, 'and before we pulled into the station at Washington, D.C., I got on my knees and accepted Christ.'

"After the meeting I said, 'Let me see that booklet.' Sure enough, stamped on the back cover was 'Pacific Garden Mission.'"

In his early years Harry Saulnier was shy. Until he was 23, he was not prepared to be a witness. Born of French parents in New York City on August 19, 1902, he struggled for years trying to be religious. He could not comprehend the way of salvation though he went to Sunday school and church and even attended a Christian and Missionary Alliance boys' camp when he was eight. Night after night, in his teens, Harry stopped for an outdoor gospel meeting in Fordham Square to hear testimonies. The group distributed gospel portions, and Harry carefully gathered the New Testament library of twenty-seven books.

In his earlier years as part owner of a sign company, it appeared that Harry was destined to help light Broadway in New York rather than to beam the gospel light on South State, Chicago. But he later sold out his interests and moved with his family to Chicago in 1922 where he went to work for the Commonwealth Edison Company.

Actually, for several years Harry had passed as a Christian, having joined Edgewater Presbyterian Church soon after coming to Chicago and becoming active in Christian Endeavor. But approaching his twenty-third birthday, he questioned his relationship to God. At the Edison Company a friend Vic Cory had an abiding peace that Harry didn't have, and he kept telling Harry that he needed to "get right with God through faith in Jesus Christ."

On his twenty-third birthday, August 19, 1925, Harry begged off from work and attended a special service at North Shore Church where Cory was a member. Here, under the preaching of John Roach Stratton, then pastor of New York's Calvary Baptist Church, he came under deep conviction of sin. He returned to two evening services, but strangely, Stratton gave no invitation. Upon returning home the second night, Harry went to his room, and, without preparing for bed, knelt and began praying. "O God, I need You," was the theme of his prayer. He told God all of his troubles and confessed that he needed God to run his life. As dawn began to break, he awoke from sleep, still on his knees, with the sunlight of God's grace filling his soul for the first time. God had heard him, and he had been born again!

As he dressed for work, Harry sensed that a victory had been won. At noon he read from the New Testament he had regularly carried as a result of his interest in Christian Endeavor, the North Shore division of which he had recently become president.

"That noon it was a brand-new Book to me," Saulnier remembers. "Oh, I can still recall that first flash and first indication that something had changed, that I was different, making the Book itself different to me."

What happened after that is ably told by his longtime friend, Dr. Victor E. Cory, founder and chairman of the board of Scripture Press Publications, Inc., Wheaton, and a member of the board of trustees of the Mission:

"From the time of his conversion, Harry began to dig out the great spiritual truths of the Word. He attended Moody Bible Institute Evening School.

"He became a flaming leader for Christ in Christian Endeavor, serving as president of CE in Chicago. Here he got his start in open-air gospel meetings, a ministry that he loves to this day. Today, when he attends conventions of both the Gideons and Christian Business Men's Committee, men look to him to head up street meetings. His foghorn voice can be heard 'a mile,' and God has used Harry's voice and winsome way to bring countless men to the foot of the Cross in open-air meetings.

"In 1928 Harry had married my sister-in-law, Gene Beryl Tucker, and I remember that he was in jail the night after his eldest daughter, Nancy, was born—all because a policeman on the beat ran him in for conducting a street meeting! Harry spent half the night in that 'dungeon' until the captain, when informed who he was, released him.

"Harry showed himself an able leader in his years in Christian Endeavor, being the spearhead of a movement that opened up Soldier Field in 1933 for a series of great Easter sunrise services. A crowd of some 15,000 poured into the huge stadium, and the way Harry and his committee handled the first service won the respect of Soldier Field officials. As a result, the services were conducted annually by Harry and his team until 1943, when he became too busy with the Mission.

"We praise God for the day he brought Harry to head up the Mission. He came as an energetic man with a mop of black hair. Today he's as energetic as ever for the Lord, though with a mop of white hair. To me Harry Saulnier is one of the wisest of God's servants, based on the verse in Proverbs: 'He that winneth souls is wise.' "

Since his Christian Endeavor days, Saulnier has enjoyed street-meeting work as much as the average layman might enjoy a round of golf. For many years he led meetings a half block from the Mission at State and Harrison where he first met Ben Engstrom. Street meetings are no game with him. They are serious business. Some years ago at a night street meeting at Kenmore and Lawrence, on Chicago's North Side, he felt constrained to cup his hands and yell at the top of his voice, "Anybody else want to be saved? If you do, stick your head out of your window, or otherwise let us know." He paused and looked about through the darkness but saw no movement. Suddenly a man stepped from a parked car. The group holding the service had no idea that anyone was even in the car, but the man said he had been listening and wanted to be saved. Saulnier says that this taught him a lesson: "You can never tell when someone might be listening to the gospel at a street meeting. Never give up; never leave a stone unturned."

At annual gatherings of the Gideons, the Christian Business Men's Committee, and the International Union of Gospel Missions, Saulnier—when he is present, as he often is—invariably leads the street meetings. In Savannah, Georgia, a handsome young couple were saved at a Saulnier-led street meeting. During a Gideon convention a fellow Gideon sidled up to Saulnier and pressed a 10 dollar bill into his hand. "Harry, use it as God would have you. You'll never know what you've meant to me." Saulnier looked at him amazed because he had no idea he had had any influence on the man whatever. The man explained that he had been in a number of street meetings which Saulnier had led, and this experience had helped to bring him out of his religious shell to the point that he himself was willing now to participate in outdoor meetings and to witness boldly for the Lord.

In Mission meetings themselves Saulnier shows himself master of every situation, it seems. He pleads tenderly and urgently for the lost to come to the Saviour and seems always to know the newcomers in the audience from the old-timers. In testimony meetings, a regular Saturday night event in the Old Lighthouse, the Lighthouse keeper is in his glory, encouraging new converts, as well as seasoned veterans, to share what Christ has done for them. One dear man became extremely emotional one evening, walking up and down an aisle shouting about what God had done for him. As he finished and sat down, all eyes turned upon Saulnier, who was leaning very patiently upon the pulpit. Unruffled, he smiled and roared, "Amen! Well, it's certainly better to shout than doubt."

Though his close friends generally concede that Saulnier's homiletics leave much to be desired, his tenacious allegiance to the fundamentals of the Word and manner of speaking have caused at least one person to compare him with the late William R. Newell, a widely known preacher, Bible teacher, and author of yesteryear. And, indeed, Saulnier in his years of growing up in the faith admired Newell and followed his teaching closely. Even to this day he promotes Newell's verse-by-verse study books in Romans, Hebrews, and Revelation. In 1952 Saulnier visited Xenia, Ohio, and Earl Eavey, head of a grocery chain, heard him speak, and later wrote the famed Bible teacher about Saulnier's resemblance to him:

"When William R. Newell goes Home, he 'still speaketh.' One of his dear friends and students, one Harry Saulnier, has been with us for the past two days. He spoke by proxy for

W. R. Newell five times in Xenia, and he certainly is the above named gentleman over and over and over again. He told the people exactly the things you would have told them, in the same tone of voice. When speaking of our identification with Christ, he yelled out, 'You are DEAD to sin. You died with Him on the Cross. You are ENLIFED with Him.' Really, Mr. Newell, it was uncanny the resemblance between Harry Saulnier and yourself in the pulpit. He looks like you, he talks like you, he acts like you, he hollers like you."

As busy as he is, Saulnier is never too busy to pray. If he is hurrying to a deputation meeting, or even just going to the drug store, he prays before starting his car, asking God to protect and guide. At a CBMC convention in Montreal in 1963, according to Charles F. Steinhofer, of Hackensack, New Jersey, Saulnier witnessed to a cabdriver. Then halfway up the steps of a restaurant into which he and the Steinhofers were hurrying, he turned and said, "Let's pray for that cabbie." And while people were waiting behind them, he prayed aloud briefly for the soul of the cabdriver.

Each day Saulnier is in close touch with God about Mission problems, and under his leadership the staff gathers every Tuesday morning for an extended prayer session in addition to the regular prayer schedule of three times a day and more. One problem he and the staff prayed long and hard about regarded the possibility of the city's taking over part of the Mission for erection of the new Jones Commercial High School. For a time it appeared that hard work of the past would be suddenly nullified. But prayer was answered, asserts Saulnier, as the Mission was left intact and the school bought property adjacent to the Old Lighthouse. It's no wonder that one of his favorite booklets, which he often has offered to Mission friends through the *PGM News,* is E. M. Bounds' *Power Through Prayer.*

Man of God that he is, Saulnier nonetheless has his rough edges. Some he probably isn't aware of; others he deeply recognizes. Sometimes, because he is naturally a high-pitched personality, he appears impatient with those with whom he works as the pressure builds up. Once an admirer wrote him that he had the face of an angel as she heard him preach in her church. An employee chuckled as the letter lay on his desk, for at that moment he was "acting like a bear." He could delegate work more than he does, some of his close associates agree, but Saulnier, dog for work that he is, often would rather do it himself than possibly have someone muff the job. Some things he insists on doing because he feels "it is the superintendent's job"— for instance, signing receipts for all gifts. At the bottom of each he writes "Hallelujah!" and a Scripture reference. Some have dubbed him "Hallelujah Harry" because of his fondness for this term of praise.

I asked Ben Engstrom, at the Mission for 21 years, to give his candid opinion of Saulnier. "Harry has the biggest sort of heart," Ben began. "Sometimes he talks big and tough, but he's the first to step in and put a compassionate arm around a man in need. Maybe one of the men will get disgusted with a Skid Row man and tell him he's been around too much. Harry, stumbling into such a situation, will, with good reasons, bring the man back in and urge the men to be patient. 'After all, the Lord is patient with us,' he says. 'Where would we be if that wasn't the case?' This is real God-given patience and love."

Because of his knowledge of rescue mission work, Saulnier has often been called on by others for counsel. The Rev. Truman Thompson, superintendent of the Denver Rescue Mission, says, " 'Iron sharpeneth iron; so a man sharpeneth the countenance of his friend.' I have sought the counsel of this man of God many times. He is warm and sympathetic, but is firm in his convictions. My heart has been encouraged and my ministry enriched through the times of fellowship I have had with him."

In early 1965 Saulnier was called to Anchorage, Alaska, by Grant Speicher and members of the local Christian Business Men's Committee to help them in launching a rescue mission ministry. In recent years one of the best-known missions, drifting into mere social work through visionless leadership at the board level, got back into the soul-winning business as Saulnier was asked to come with his doctor's kit.

At PGM Saulnier looks to a godly board of businessmen to oversee the Mission program, some of them the same men who elected him to the superintendency in 1940. "Without dedicated godly laymen at the top guiding a rescue mission, it's so easy for a good work to crumble," Harry asserts. Working with him on the board of trustees are: Roy Baumann, Caspar F. Henning, J. Paul Bennett, M.D., Russell G. Johnson, Richard B. Stanley, Carl H. Johnson, Paul C. Benson, Clayton F. Brown, Victor E. Cory, John C. Ewing, Herbert C. Hansen, Charles B. Jensen, Philip A. Lind, Lorne H. Renner, and H. G. Swanson, Sr. For many years a trustee and close adviser was Freelin A. Carlton, manager of the huge State Street Sears store, who some years ago moved to Arizona. He and Frank E. Sandberg, a retired businessman living in Florida, are trustees emeritus of the Mission.

Saulnier's own family stand solidly behind him in his ministry at the Old Lighthouse. His wife, Gene, works closely with the Women's Auxiliary and conducts deputation meetings from time to time. She also does personal work at the Mission. For some years the Saulniers' eldest child, tall, sturdy David, from the same mold as his father, helped lead singing at the Mission and worked as film secretary. He now plays and sings in a gospel quartet that ministers regularly in churches and missions, known as "The Westerners." Nancy is vice-president in a brokerage office in the Chicago Board of Trade Building and often visits the Mission. Carol, the youngest member of the family, is a "homebody."

Lance B. Latham, Saulnier's pastor, thanks God for Harry's faithfulness as a member and Sunday school teacher at the North Side Gospel Center. "I can see very easily how a person in his position could latch on to some rich church where he would get a lot of help for the Mission, but I believe Harry, ever true to the Lord, prefers to go where he has fellowship with the Lord and loves the message and our trying to stay to God's ways of doing the work of the Lord," says Latham. "I just feel that I am doing just about nothing when I stand alongside of him and see the wonderful vision and work God has given him. I just noticed last Sunday when he was so faithfully taking one of our older men home after the service, seeing a person sitting on a bench across the street, he took time out and talked to him about the Lord. I am sure he is not after the big things; he is after the hearts of men."

Dr. Walter L. Wilson, the "beloved physician" from Kansas City, Missouri, summed up Harry Saulnier with this comment: "My precious Brother Saulnier is a walking advertisement for our Lord Jesus and a constant example of the presence and power of the Holy Spirit."

Chapter 11

GOOD-BYE, SKID ROW!

SKID ROW as a state of existence is as old as man, beginning with the skid in the Garden. Happily, by love and grace, God made a way back for Adam and Eve, clothing them in coats of skin and promising a Redeemer. However, rejecting the way of faith, their son Cain walked Skid Row "a fugitive and vagabond in the earth" (Gen. 4:14). Later, even godly Noah fell victim to wine and spent at least an evening on Skid Row. Weak-faithed Lot lived for years on the Row, and the last glimpse of him after he fled Sodom before its destruction reveals him in a drunken, immoral state. There were, of course, many others in Old Testament times who partially or fully lived a Skid Row existence.

In New Testament times, in the country of the Gadarenes, a man with an unclean spirit dwelt among the tombs—Skid Row, first-century style. No man could tame him. Then Jesus came. By His power, the man was transformed in an instant! People came out to see what had happened. They simply could not believe their eyes, for now the madman of the tombs was "sitting, and clothed, and in his right mind" (Mark 5:15).

Jesus compassionately loved the Skid Row people of His day, and wherever He went He ministered to them. He dealt tenderly with the sin-stained woman at the well. Significantly, the first person to whom He appeared following His resurrection was none other than Mary Magdalene, out of whom He had cast seven devils!

It is this same divine power—Christ's matchless power to transform man at his worst—that for nearly a century has made the Pacific Garden Mission so much more than a mere social service agency. For over the years men and women, suddenly free of harrassing demons and binding cords of sin, have in great numbers gone from the Old Lighthouse each year whole and in their right minds and back to a useful place in society. In addition to the many who have heard the call of God into special Christian service, countless others have gone home to parents, wives, husbands, children, and sweethearts. They have rolled up their sleeves and returned to work to support their families and have become reliable workers and respected citizens of their communities and churches.

That isn't to say that none has ever slipped. Some have slipped as badly as Noah. Then there are always those whose faith is weak or even nonexistent, floundering souls like Lot who escaped Skid Row city but who when last heard of had fallen again to a miserable state. A case in point is "Bill," who came to Pacific Garden Mission to grow spiritual legs after he had testified to "a wonderful transformation in my life" while in prison. He talked of continuing his studies at Moody Bible Institute, but he never got around to it. Later he drifted away, became a carnival worker, a junk picker, and a hard drinker. One day he was found shot to death in the snow outside his home, a dilapidated shack near a junkyard outside of Western Springs, Illinois.

Evidently in Bill's case the gospel seed had fallen among thorns. Such heartaches go with any soul-winning effort, but happily there are many who represent good ground, who keep the Word and bring forth fruit.

A man from Sacramento, California, returned home a few years ago after being lifted by Christ from Skid Row. A little later he wrote the Mission: "I called my wife. We met and had a good talk, and God was there also. We worked everything out, except what I was going to do about a job. But God had that figured out, too, because Saturday morning I got a job on a ranch with a good salary. Within a month or two, we can get our debts straightened out. So we are praising God and walking with Him, and we are praying for His guidance in our lives."

Though Elmer Medek was never a down-and-outer, drink and self ruled his life. But all changed June 25, 1960, the night he came with his wife to the Mission upon the invitation of a friend.

In the Mission meeting, Medek, hearing the gospel, saw his sins from God's viewpoint, and that night he and his wife both received Christ. How much of a difference did it make in Elmer's life? Three days before I wrote this chapter, Bob Schultz, branch manager for a large lumber company in the Chicago area, told me of hearing Elmer Medek's story on PGM's "Unshackled!" radio series. He had worked with an Elmer Medek thirty years before, and he wondered if he was the same man whose story had been told over the airwaves. Knowing Harry Saulnier, he phoned him and obtained Medek's phone number.

"Are you the same Elmer Medek I worked with in Villa Park?" Schultz asked, after identifying himself.

"Yep, that's me."

A revealing conversation followed, and Schultz has since seen Medek on a number of occasions.

"Why, I remember him as one of the most selfish persons I've ever known—a completely despicable character, the kind of guy few people could stand," Schultz commented. "Now he's entirely changed. Often Medek gives his testimony at the Mission on Saturday night meetings. Has a good job—is assistant purchasing agent for an electrical firm in Chicago."

Believe it or not, Carl Graden took his first step toward Skid Row when he was but eight years of age. "No son of mine is going to grow up without being able to hold his liquor like a man!" his father boasted, and he gave Carl a man-sized drink.

Years later, living in Rockford, Illinois, Carl Graden depended so much on liquor that even his dad's horrible, violent death from alcoholic poisoning failed to shake the bottle loose from Carl's hand. Then, after a complete nervous breakdown, Carl's mother was dead too, heartbroken over the way alcohol had ruined her family.

During these days, oddly enough, Carl Graden contributed to his church, and went regularly to Sunday morning services—when he wasn't too hung over. His minister tried to turn him from his drinking but with no success. One thing, however, stuck with Graden: a story about a drunk who walked into the Pacific Garden Mission.

Ultimately, Graden hit Skid Row, Chicago. On the night of January 11, 1944, when he was 43, Graden blacked out in the snow. When he came to, he walked into the Mission to get help. That night Graden trusted the Saviour and the miracle of redemption took place inside. The fetters and chains that had shackled him were broken.

Carl Graden later left Chicago and married. His wife, Ruth, became a Christian after she saw the change Christ had made in Carl. Until his death in 1964, in a traffic accident, he was a barber in Seattle, Washington, and active in a church in Bothell, Washington.

George Mohr always claimed it was the prayers of his little German mother that ultimately brought him to the Mission and gave him a new start in life. She died when George was a boy and he began a lonely existence. Unfortunately in his late teen years he began depending on liquor like his mother had depended on praying. In the years that followed he married and had five children. His wife, Sally, remained patient with him as he drifted through one job to another, from one drunk to another.

Ultimately, Mohr left his family and became an alcohol-soaked derelict. In an empty boxcar or sleeping on the ground in some Skid Row alley he'd hear his mother praying for him and cry. Once he fell asleep with his legs across a rail on a siding. Next morning an empty coach had rolled in and stopped six inches from his legs! God must have been remembering the prayers of his little German mother.

Soon after that Mohr went to work in a government camp in Muskegon, Michigan, and for the first time in eight years he wrote home to the family. A few days later he got a letter from his daughter, Ruth. He had been on an all-night binge, but then, as if a cold knife had been jabbed into his brain, he sobered up. For black as death before his eyes were words like these: "My heart is too heavy to write much. Mother died suddenly yesterday evening. She was drawing water at the kitchen sink. . . ."

Not long after that, beaten and whipped, Mohr landed in Chicago in 1940 and staggered into the Pacific Garden Mission. A sign in the window said, "Mother's prayers follow you." In the Mission prayer room that night, George knelt with Harry Saulnier. "I know you're drunk, George, but God can get to you," Saulnier said gently, as if he was talking to a child. "When you say the word, He can get through!"

God did get through and a mother's prayers were answered. Eleven years later, in the *Pacific Garden Mission News,* George testified:

"Now, I'm filled and satisfied and happy, no longer drifting or hunting anymore. The Pacific Garden Mission gave me medical care for a solid year, and now I'm living!" Mohr, who lived in Cleveland, died a few years ago in his eighties.

Leonard Pollari, born of Finnish parents, earned the title of "black sheep" as he let liquor run his life and run him right out of the Army. In 1947 he hit Skid Row, Chicago, and one night wandered into the Mission, where the smile and testimony of a Jewish man and then the smile and testimony of a sailor impressed him. Later he ran into an old buddy who also had a smile—and a testimony too. He invited Pollari back to the Mission, and there he made a profession of faith in Christ. But, neglecting Christian fellowship, Pollari slipped back to drinking. Then he returned to the Old Lighthouse and renewed fellowship with Christ and His people. For a year he lived the life then slipped again. Later, back at the Mission, Pollari talked with Harry Saulnier, and he suggested that Pollari truly make Christ the center of his life and soak up more of God's Word. Today, after working in Chicago for several years, Lenny Pollari is still a man with a smile and a testimony, employed as a repairman in Lewistown, Illinois. He is married, has two children, and is active in a local church.

A man who will long be remembered at the Old Lighthouse is Howard La Bounty, a pitiful human wreck who was towed into the Mission one June afternoon in the early 1950's by his sister, Mabel Pulaski, who had compassionately searched for him on Skid Row after his mother and then his father had died heartbroken over his condition. La Bounty, a truck driver for 31 years before succumbing to drink, came into the Mission like a whipped, dirty stray dog. He had been sleeping in boxcars, under trees, in alleys. Haakon Evans, then assistant superintendent, who tenderly took charge, recalls La Bounty vividly:

"In my years in mission work, I have never seen another person in Howard La Bounty's condition. His thick gray hair was long and matted and his tattered clothing was slick with grease and filth. His eyes were blank and he could barely mumble."

Someone put La Bounty under a shower and scrubbed him, then shaved him, washed and cut his hair and gave him clean clothes. Then he was given food and taken to the evening service. That night he became a new creature in Christ. He became a wonderfully transformed person as the love of God motivated his life in the years that followed. One time, as he assisted in the work at the Mission, he was viciously bitten on a finger by a crazed derelict. For many weeks he was hospitalized. Later, back on the job La Bounty had a decision to make. Haakon Evans told him that the man who had attacked him was upstairs in the Mission. "Would it bother you if we let the man come down here to the dining hall where you are working?"

"Why, bring him on down and we'll feed him, Mr. Evans. God forgave me. Why shouldn't I forgive that man?" La Bounty said in the sweet way that typified him after he became a Christian.

La Bounty helped at the Mission for several years, then took a job elsewhere, continuing to walk with Christ. He died three years ago.

Hundreds of other stories of men helped by the Skid Row division of the Mission could be told. Each would be as amazing as the next, as much a miracle as the marvelous transformation of the wild man of the tombs in the land of the Gadarenes. For, after all, the same Saviour touched them all.

Chapter 12

CALLED TO SERVE

AMONG THE CLEAR INDICATIONS that God's hand of blessing has rested in power on the historic Old Lighthouse year after year is the fact that hosts of its converts have gone into some phase of full-time Christian service. And this is amazing when you consider that most of these people got a miserable start in life and were once the worst sort of sinners.

Today some of the key people who help keep the light of the Old Lighthouse itself gleaming brightly are men who themselves experienced the miracle of a transformed life in the Mission.

By the time he was 14, Arnold Vander Meulen had been in criminal court twice and was an alcoholic. By the time he was 16, he had been in and out of jail several places over the U.S., and at that age became the youngest boy ever sentenced to the Southern Michigan Prison. His mother practically broke down when the sentence was pronounced. But she and his father, both praying Christians, held on to God for Arnold's salvation.

Arnold tells the remainder of his story in these words:

"I served three years, got out, and once again bummed around the country, drinking, taking dope, fighting. Then came Pearl Harbor and the draft. But even in uniform I refused to have any relation with God. Twice I deserted. When arrested, I slugged my guard and escaped.

"Now I was a fugitive for sure. Sometimes as I went from state to state I heard from the folks back home in Grand Rapids, Michigan, and always it was the same thing: 'God can save you from the uttermost to the uttermost, Arnold. We love you, Son. You're all wrapped up in prayer.'

"I shrugged off every reminder of my sin and of God until on New Year's Eve 1947 I took a cheap peek at my life and felt sick. I was in a dive on South State Street in Chicago. It was nearly 11:00—only one more hour of 1947 left. And somehow for the first time in my life I was scared! I wished I could run home and cry on Mom's shoulder. But I couldn't; so I began walking, hoping the cold night air would help. Soon I was looking up into the big sign in front of Pacific Garden Mission: 'JESUS SAVES.' I had laughed at those words on missions over the country, but now they gripped me.

"The Mission doorman invited me in, and I sat down in the back, sobbing. I hunted through my pockets until I found the prayer Dad left me last time he had visited me in jail. From a crumpled piece of paper, I read: 'God be merciful to me a sinner, and save me now, for Jesus' sake!'

"And with that, as I turned my back on sin and my face to the Son of God, I became a new creature and new desires took the place of the old ones. No one had said a word to me. Prayers had done it all!

"Some time later, still at the Mission, I was wondering what to do about my past crimes. To give myself up would mean years in prison. But God knew about my weakness and took the whole matter into His own hands! For a man came up to me and said:

" 'F.B.I. You're under arrest.'

"In Superior Court in Grand Rapids I was arraigned on a charge of forgery and got two to fourteen years in the Southern Michigan Prison, to which I had been sentenced when I was sixteen.

"In prison I was invited to teach a Bible class. Over the months it grew from a handful to some 600 members. Another miracle took place as the Army, hearing of my new life, dropped charges for desertion and made me eligible to collect enough bonus money to pay for my bad checks: $153.50, the amount I owed to the penny!

"Then came that day nineteen months after my imprisonment when the warden announced: " 'Arnold, the parole board says you can leave us. This time we hate to see you go. But God bless you. I know He will.' "

God's blessings on Arnold Vander Meulen are evidenced by the fact he has been used to found rescue missions in Grand Rapids, his hometown; Bristol, Virginia; and Battle Creek, Michigan. He returned to Pacific Garden Mission in 1960 to direct its deputation ministry. In a recent year his teams have preached in 400 services to approximately 65,000 people, resulting in some 900 professions of faith in Christ. Vander Meulen himself is often engaged to preach. He is on the road across the U.S. and Canada representing the Mission about 40 weeks a year, preaching and giving his testimony in prisons, service club meetings, church gatherings, and on radio and TV.

In the late '40's in Peoria, Illinois, a tavern owner opened his place one morning only to find that thieves had broken in during the night. Suddenly he saw that one was still there in a drunken stupor from beverages he had guzzled. The owner began to beat the man, Augustus Hollis, shellacking him from wall to wall. Later in the county jail, bruised and groggy, Hollis tried to take his life by hanging himself with his belt.

The suicide attempt resulted in his being sent to the state hospital for the criminally insane for two years. Then, when Hollis was released, he drew two to four years in the state prison for the burglary charge.

In 1961 Gus slouched over a wine bottle in Boots' Tavern, then two doors from Pacific Garden Mission. By now he was fast on his way toward becoming a Skid Row fixture, though in past years he had been paid well as a pantryman in a private club. Suddenly in his foggy state he heard snatches of words from a song, "No one ever cared for me like Jesus." The song was coming from the loudspeaker of the Mission and was being sung by Ruth Smiley.

Gus stumbled into the Mission. A personal worker came to him with a warm word of greeting and asked him to go to the prayer room for counseling and prayer.

"No," Gus mumbled, "not now—I've got two bottles of wine in my pocket, and where I go the bottles go." Pulling away, Gus said he would talk some other time.

Gus tells the remainder of the story:

"I returned the next day and the gentleman showed me from the Bible where I was wrong and how Christ could change my life to be a useful one. I professed the Lord, but for the first months I stumbled and slipped away.

"Then, in desperation, I came back to the Mission and talked with someone else. I told him what had happened.

" 'Gus,' he explained, 'you must give your *all* to the Lord. You can't carry the load yourself. You tried and failed. Each morning pray, asking the Lord to carry you through the day. He says, "Ask, and it shall be given you. Knock, and it shall be opened unto you." '

"I followed his advice, and the Lord began giving me complete victory over the sin that had dragged me down. He has kept me from drink. I have my trust in Him, because I no longer trust myself."

Today barrel-chested Gus Hollis, using the talent he developed while serving in the Merchant Marine in the early 1940's, serves the Lord full time at the Old Lighthouse as chief cook, heading up a kitchen crew of 15. He is responsible for meals served to Skid Row men and others helped by the Mission, as well as meals for the staff.

Chief custodian and head of the work crew at the Old Lighthouse is a lean, lanky young man with dark hair and dark eyes. His name: Robert Vehue. To see him today you would never dream that on at least three occasions Bob cheated death in situations brought on by alcoholism.

Once, in Latin America, he went on a drinking binge and ended up swallowing a dozen sleeping pills. A friend rushed him to a hospital where he was nursed back to health.

Later, back in the States, in a drunken condition he made a smart remark to a gang of young men. They chased him until they cornered him and beat him to within an inch of his life.

Under treatment for the wounds suffered in the attack, Bob began going through horrible suffering as the result of sudden withdrawal of liquor. He was headed for delirium tremens.

It seemed that the whole world was against him. Voices taunted him. Suddenly one night Bob grabbed a glass water carafe from his bed table, smashed it, and plunged the jagged glass deep into his throat.

Bob began to run and found himself standing on a roof, rain pouring down and blood covering him. And there, glowing in the dark, it seemed that he saw the grinning, staring face of Satan!

Out of the hospital later, he went on his last drunk. When it was over he was penniless and homeless. A policeman directed him to Pacific Garden Mission where the Holy Spirit moved in his heart and brought him into a personal relationship with Jesus Christ. The desire for drink has vanished and peace rules Bob's heart as he directs the work of keeping the Old Lighthouse bright and clean.

Undoubtedly one of the most refreshing personalities serving the Lord at the Mission is none other than the ex-steel mill foreman saved from a life of alcoholism in 1945 through the preaching and personal work of Harry Saulnier—curly-haired, aged Ben Engstrom. Serving as building engineer, he cares for electrical equipment and keeps radiators hot when temperatures sag during wintry months. Ben has had the joy of sharing his story with thousands, in magazines, on the radio, and in meetings both at the mission, in Chicagoland churches, and elsewhere as he has traveled with PGM deputation teams.

Among those who have been saved and fired up at the Mission to go elsewhere to serve is Jack Martin. As a youth, he struck out on his own, the victim of a broken home. At 14, he worked with a carnival, doubling as a cook and washer and doing the bally for the "world-famous" glassblower. When he was 15, Jack found that a few good stiff drinks kept him from getting tired from the two jobs and made him more a part of the rollicking carnival crew.

As the years passed, Jack drank steadily and ultimately became enmeshed in gambling. As troubles weighed upon him, he turned to marihuana.

In 1947, by this time unable to sit still five minutes without a cigarette or a drink, he landed in Chicago. One day, being stabbed by stomach pains and tired of killing time looking at movies, Jack strolled past the corner of Harrison and State. Suddenly he stopped. A crowd was watching a big man doing a coin trick. But when he began talking about the most wonderful Gift in the world, Jack realized the man was a preacher. Yet he stayed and listened, and even raised his hand for prayer when the big man said he'd pray for those who had a need. Jack wanted prayer—for his stomachache.

After the street service the big man approached Jack. "My name's Pete Tanis—I'm from the Pacific Garden Mission. Now that I've prayed *for* you, I want to pray *with* you."

Later, living temporarily at the Mission on Tanis' invitation, Jack Martin pretended that he was a Christian, helping out in the kitchen and attending gospel services and Bible classes. Then one day as Edward Ockert, former athletic coach at Moody Bible Institute, taught the Converts' Bible Class, Jack opened his heart to the Saviour and became a new creation.

At the Mission Jack met Jo Young, a former model who had come to Christ in a Youth for Christ rally, and some months later they were married. With a God-given desire to be used to win others to Christ, they served for a time at the famous Keswick Colony of Mercy in New Jersey, helping bring the gospel to alcoholics. Later Jack became superintendent of the

City Rescue Mission in Peoria, Illinois. In 1963, Jack and Jo, with their three sons and their daughter, moved to Spokane, Washington, where Jack today directs the Union Gospel Mission.

John Fink in more ways than one followed in the footsteps of Jack Martin. By the time he was 14, he had learned to drink and was earning his own money doing a mechanical man act on the famous Boardwalk in Atlantic City, New Jersey. When he was 16, he considered suicide because drink had gotten a viselike grip on him.

John tried the Navy, but drunkenness and undisciplined conduct resulted in his discharge. Leaving Great Lakes Naval Training Station north of Chicago, he came to Chicago and began a tour of honky-tonks and saloons. He was fairly drunk when he drifted out of a tattoo parlor and stood on the sidewalk, wondering what to do next. Up the street a red neon sign blazed out the message, "JESUS SAVES—PACIFIC GARDEN MISSION."

That night John Fink came to heckle, but instead he got under conviction as he heard the gospel. One Scripture verse stuck with him: "Believe on the Lord Jesus Christ, and thou shalt be saved" (Acts 16:31). That night, a Gideon Bible in his hand, he knelt beside his bed in his hotel room and put his trust in Christ. Delivered from sin and the curse of alcohol, John Fink served for a time as a counselor in the Old Lighthouse and in 1964 went to Atlantic City where he founded and became the first superintendent of the newly formed Atlantic City Rescue Mission.

Over the years scores of other PGM converts have gone into some phase of mission work, either as helpers or superintendents. In 1884 "Curly" Tom Mackay, son of a saloonkeeper and he himself a panhandler and alcoholic, came to Christ in the Mission and later became head of Los Angeles' Helping Hand Mission and a great open-air preacher on the West Coast. He was probably the first PGM convert to head another mission, though

Harry Monroe and Mel Trotter were the most famous mission workers among those saved at PGM.

Percy E. Diehl learned to drink as a boy in Traverse City, Mich., and had one foot in hell the night he came to the Mission in the 1930's. Today he and his wife, Albina, assist in the work at the Olive Branch Mission on Madison Street, Chicago.

Clyde Parker, a Missouri boy who became a gambler and boozer, swung on crutches into the Mission on April 22, 1956. Today he helps win souls in the Bible Rescue Mission on Madison Street in Chicago.

In addition to mission workers, the Old Lighthouse has produced a host of preachers, evangelists, chaplains, and missionaries. Besides Billy Sunday, among the old-timers are such men as Robert Atchison, a tramp who found Christ in 1893 in the Mission and went out as a missionary to the Orient and became known as the "Mueller of Japan" and the "Mikado." George Preston was another. His mother's prayers reached from Northern Ireland to Chicago in 1910 and George responded to the invitation of Harry Monroe to receive Christ. A gifted singer who sang on the operatic and theatrical stage, Preston later became an evangelist, preaching and singing the gospel until his death in 1941.

Others include Billy Driver, the Scot who laid down his carpenter's tools to serve as an evangelist till his death in 1927; Lew Speegle, the street fakir, who became a lay evangelist in Wisconsin; Martin O'Connor, the liquor-loving plumber who, by God's power, threw away the bottle to become a missionary evangelist in northern Wisconsin; John Troy, son of a famous European physician who found himself penniless and friendless in Chicago, then received Christ at the Mission in 1908 and went out as a much-traveled evangelist; Elias Auger, a drifter who found an anchor in Christ in 1899 and for more than thirty years was a Baptist minister and chaplain; Elmer Wagler, who trusted Christ in 1921 and overcame a stuttering tongue to preach the gospel and become head of the Southern

Highland Evangel; Royal L. Leeson, a Skid Row resident saved in 1924 who went to Latin America as a missionary; and George Quilty, who once thought that anyone who wasn't a Jew was a Christian until he encountered Christ in the Mission in 1921 and became a lay preacher as he continued his work at Western Electric Company.

Countless people already trusting Christ for salvation have been fired up at the Mission and have gone out in fruitful service. Holland Oates, saved from a life of drunkenness shortly after the death of his infant daughter, was a "settled" Christian when he visited the Old Lighthouse soon after World War I, a row of cigars displayed in his coat pocket. A personal worker talked to him about giving himself wholly to God, and this was a step toward Oates' becoming an itinerant preacher among the farmers of Wisconsin until his death in 1939. Another who came to the place of complete surrender at the Mission is John R. Rice, today a famed evangelist. The night he came to the Mission in May 1921 he saw sinners, almost hopeless in their despair, find forgiveness and peace. That night he promised God that "if He could help me save sinners, He could have me to preach to sinners. Thus," Dr. Rice says, "I became a preacher of the gospel of Christ."

October 8, 1931, found Arthur E. Petznick, who had left home at 20, sitting in a pool room on the corner of State and Harrison in Chicago. When policemen came in the front door, Petznick ducked out a side door into a cold drizzle. Friendless and penniless, he faced another night on a park bench. As he was passing the Old Lighthouse, the doorman handed him a tract and invited him inside. Petznick tells the rest:

"The first thing that greeted my eyes was a sign on the wall which asked: 'HOW LONG SINCE YOU WROTE TO MOTHER?' In five years I had not so much as sent her a card. I relived my childhood days and saw how I had dishonored and disgraced my mother. Oh, I was miserable. Then I heard Dad Taylor preach the gospel as I never heard it before. The invitation was given. I raised my hand and a personal worker came and took me into the prayer room. There I cried to God from the depth of a broken heart, and God heard me. And His dear Son came to abide in me."

Arthur Petznick soon entered Moody Bible Institute, graduated, and became a pastor. For many years he has pastored the Bible Baptist Church in Phoenix, Arizona.

Time and space fail in the telling of others. For many books could be written of the long parade of those who met the Saviour at Pacific Garden Mission, rose from ruined lives, and in the power of their new Lord went forth to unfurl the gospel banner in Satan's strongholds throughout the world.

Chapter 13

A HAVEN FOR WOMEN

POLICE, while engaged in a routine investigation of a stabbing in an apartment building on Chicago's West Side, discover a Puerto Rican family living in unimaginable filth and destitution. Garbage litters the living room and the baby, naked except for a heavy coat swathed around him, lies on a stained mattress. The sole furnishings of the room are two incredibly dirty mattresses and a chair. Four other children appear sickly and neglected. The mother is mentally retarded, the father in prison serving 199 years for murder. The family needs help—*now.*

A dejected woman, looking middle-aged rather than just 35, walks unsteadily down a street south of Chicago's Loop area. Once a respected office worker but now a victim of drink and dope, she needs a real friend in the worst sort of way.

A 26-year-old wife of a sailor traveling from California to Great Lakes Naval Training Station arrives in Chicago where a man snatches her purse containing her money, bus tickets, and baggage check. Frightened and alone, she too needs a loving hand extended to her.

Actual cases, all of these represent problems faced around the clock 12 months a year in big, bustling Chicago. In the heartrending situation involving the Puerto Rican family, police brought the mother and her five children to Pacific Garden Mission's Women's and Children's Division where they were given care and some days later turned over to grandparents. As for the 35-year-old alcoholic and dope addict, she was welcomed, and a supervisor lovingly cared for her and tucked her into a clean bed for her first restful night's sleep in weeks. The sailor's wife was given overnight lodging, her baggage was obtained, and next day she was sent on to her husband.

But best of all, in each of these cases, the women were counseled directly from God's Word and, with the exception of the Puerto Rican mother, who was mentally retarded, each responded to God's love and eagerly opened her heart to Jesus Christ before leaving the Mission.

This, briefly, is the 24-hour, seven-day-a-week job of the Women's and Children's Division of the Old Lighthouse, one of the few shelters in Chicago where women and children are welcomed into a homey atmosphere and at the same time are told of the One who once said, "Come unto me, all ye that labour and are heavy laden, and I will give you rest" (Matt. 11:28). Annually as many as 6400, including individual women and mothers and children, are guests of the Mission. Night after night the Division's ten beds are occupied and often children must sleep on couches and on mattresses on the floor.* Since many individuals and families stay at the Mission over a period of several days—some for several weeks—there is much exposure to spiritual counseling, resulting in a high percentage of professions of faith in the Saviour. In one recent year 109 decisions for Christ were recorded.

The vision for the women's work of PGM was given by God to Mrs. Susan Wymer, a godly soul winner who today, even in the twilight years of life, continues her weekly visits to Dwight Reformatory for Women in Dwight, Illinois, to point delinquent girls to a new life in Jesus Christ. One day in 1941 Mrs. Wymer, with a friend, called on Harry Saulnier and jolted him with, "Mr. Saulnier, we've been thinking about getting a women's work started here. We need a division of the work where women of the street can come and be dealt with.

---

*As this was written, the Women's and Children's Division was being enlarged so that 50 beds could be added. Plans were also being made to house waifs and other children not accompanied by at least one parent or guardian.

There are so many girls wandering the streets who need the Saviour."

Pieces fell together in jigsaw-puzzle fashion as Saulnier thought about it. For a long time he had been bothered by the lack of adequate means of dealing with women needing spiritual counseling.

"Mrs. Wymer, we don't have any money right now for this kind of work, but go ahead. Do what you can. We'll trust the Lord for this just like we trust Him for everything else. Amen?" Saulnier didn't know it then, but he had just made one of the major decisions that would take Pacific Garden Mission one step closer to becoming a model big-city soul-winning station.

At first the ministry consisted mainly of counseling. But as God began supplying extra funds, the staff prepared and furnished the second floor, and later the third floor, of one of the two additional buildings the Mission had obtained in November 1941. By late 1943 a sign was hung out welcoming needy women and offering overnight accommodations. Here was a relatively new approach to rescue mission work—one destined to pay off in great dividends in souls won to Christ.

Miss Grace Vander Ploeg, a Chicagoan working as a missionary in Paterson, New Jersey, came to head up the new division. In her nine years with the Mission, she became acquainted with the girls of the burlesque shows and taverns on South State. Some of them would wind up in Women's Court and appeal to her to get them out again.

Eventually Miss Vander Ploeg was spending almost as much time in court as at the Mission, so in 1950 she left, believing that God wanted her to work full-time at the Court. Later she married Wilfred A. Willett. She continues in this ministry to this very day.

In Norfolk, Virginia, in 1946 God was beginning to shape another vessel for service in the Women's Division. Yeoman 2/c Elaine Chobanoff, an Elyria, Ohio, girl serving in the WAVES, met Christ through a Navigators representative.

In 1950 Elaine Chobanoff, by this time a graduate of Moody Bible Institute, was a Thursday evening volunteer worker at the Mission. During her MBI days she had become acquainted with rescue mission work, and God led her back to PGM to take Mrs. Willett's post.

Currently assisting Miss Chobanoff is Mrs. Hildred Stout, 52, a pleasant-faced widow from Pennsylvania who became interested in the work of PGM when she saw *Out of the Night,* the first PGM film, at a Bible conference more than 12 years ago. She told the Lord then that if He should someday take her husband she would like to work with women at Pacific Garden Mission. Ten years ago her husband died, but there was a long training period—helping in a nursing home for eight years—before she came to the Mission in 1964.

One Saturday morning I dropped into the Women's Division and talked with Mrs. Stout, who was then on duty. (Currently, she has night duty and Miss Chobanoff, day supervision.)

Among the women being cared for then was a 70-year-old pensioner who had checked in at 2:00 that morning.

In the living room Mrs. Stout introduced me to "Mary," a chubby, baby-faced girl of about 19 whom I took to be of Mexican descent. Her boyfriend had been arrested the night before, and police had brought her to the Mission.

Mrs. Stout ushered me to the third floor to a comfortably furnished parlor just off the kitchen of the Women's Division, and we sat and talked of recent cases. Some days before, in the same room, I had chatted with Miss Chobanoff. Both supervisors agreed that mentally unbalanced women outnumber even alcoholics among those who have found their way to the Mission during the past six years. Statistics reveal that there are some 8½ million people with serious mental difficulties in the U.S., and some experts estimate that the total may be much higher, perhaps 15 to 20 percent of the population.

Among the mentally afflicted, "Edith," an 18-year-old Negro girl, stands out in Mrs. Stout's memory. "She is a beautiful girl,"

Mrs. Stout declared. "I told Elaine, 'Believe me, she could go a long way with her appearance.' But she was so mixed up. When anybody would get in a conversation, she'd think they were talking about her. She would go into a tantrum. She would throw her hands up in the air and scream and cry and call me. Also, she apparently suffers from claustrophobia. She felt closed in and complained that the beds were too close together. One night I finally moved her out into the hall, so she could be near my bedroom and could call me if she needed me.

"One night Edith told me that she was going to go to work at 9:00 as a waitress. I picked out a nice uniform for her and patted her on the shoulder as she left. 'Edith, you look real sweet. Be a good girl now.' But after two or three nights I began to get suspicious. She was going to work at different hours, and I was getting up at 2 and 3 o'clock in the morning to let her in. Surely a restaurant wouldn't have those hours.

"Finally, I brought her up here and I counseled with her. She said she accepted the Lord. For about two days it seemed that she might be working the 6:00 to 12:00 shift, but then the hours changed again. I had another talk with her. Edith, I don't believe you're really working.'

"She put her head down, and I said, 'Have you been?'

" 'No,' she said. 'I have a friend on the North Side, and I've been staying with him.'

"Before Edith left us after several weeks, I learned from an outside source that she had had a baby before coming here, something she had withheld from us. She was startled when I mentioned that I knew about this phase of her life. I still pray for Edith, though we haven't seen her for some time."

At this point Mrs. Stout went into an adjoining room to answer a phone. I caught snatches of the conversation at our end, and the delight in Mrs. Stout's voice indicated this was one of her girls. Somehow I was not surprised when Mrs. Stout returned a moment later, smiling, and announced, "Why, that was the girl we were just talking about—Edith. She's in a mental hospital. Wants to come back and pick up some books and things she left."

Thus, Edith's story was still being written. There would be at least one more contact with her. If only somehow she would come to Jesus Christ and be unshackled.

Another type of girl who finds love and understanding at the Mission is the unmarried expectant mother—like the mentally ill, a serious problem on the national scene. Miss Chobanoff helps put these girls in touch with welfare authorities who work out details for their care. The Mission often provides maternity clothing; and before each girl leaves, she is given a layette.

The spiritual counsel and Christian love shown these frightened, frustrated girls make deep impressions. Several babies have been named for the two supervisors. One Negro girl, wanting to honor Mrs. Stout, however was troubled. "Mrs. Stout, what is your middle name?" she asked forthrightly.

"I don't have any," she replied.

"Oh, you don't."

"No, but why do you ask?"

"Oh, I wanted to name my baby after you if it's a girl, but I don't believe I like Hildred too well."

Even so, before the expectant mother went on to be hospitalized elsewhere to await her baby, she had come to like the name. Mrs. Stout never heard whether the baby was a boy or girl, but if it was a girl there's undoubtedly one additional Hildred in the world because a girl in need was taken in at the Mission.

Among alcoholics who have been helped is "Anne" whose pastor phoned the Mission from a nearby state. Anne, a 42-year-old woman from the community, needed aid desperately to break a drinking habit that had plagued her home for 18 years. Her husband had just said that he was giving up on her and would find someone to care for their little girl.

"We will be looking for her," Miss Chobanoff told the pastor.

The church people put Anne on a bus, and a few hours later

she was being put to bed in the Women's Division. She had the shakes and Mrs. Stout gave her hot coffee and aspirin. It took half a dozen more cups of coffee at intervals to get through the night.

Next morning Miss Chobanoff counseled with Anne and read to her from the Bible. That night, her mind clearer, the woman attended the service in the Mission chapel and made a profession of faith in Christ. During the next five weeks both Miss Chobanoff and Mrs. Stout helped her get established in the Word. When she appeared strong enough to return home, the Mission supervisor surprised her with a wardrobe of clothes and put her on a bus, committing her to the Lord. A letter several days later indicated that a victory had truly been won: "What surprises me," she said, "is that I can walk uptown and I can pass those taverns. I don't even want to go in!"

Later, though, when her husband got tired of a "religious, goody-good" wife, Anne slipped back to drink. But she quickly packed up again and headed back for Chicago and the Mission where she knew she would receive help and grow still stronger. As this is being written, Anne is still at the Mission.

Homeless families—some with fathers out of work, others out on the street because fathers have left home—regularly come or are sent to the Mission. One day in 1961 police deposited a mother and her five children in the Mission. Marie Harrington and her brood were living in a car, having been put in the street for failure to pay rent. The thrilling events that transpired in the days and weeks following are summarized in a letter Mrs. Harrington wrote in 1964:

"I was against staying in a mission, but was I in for surprises! Even though the Women's Division was cramped and it seemed as if children were crawling out of the woodwork, my five kids and I were made to feel at home.

"Bit by bit my antagonism was melted by the concerned workers who were always ready to take time with my troubles. And little by little the love of Christ began drawing me. It impressed me that everyone sang a hymn before we sat down to eat. One night when someone baby-sat for me, I attended the evening service, and at the invitation went forward and accepted the Lord Jesus Christ as my Saviour.

"The three weeks I stayed at the Mission changed the course of my life. The Lord Jesus promised to make everything new, and He has. Four of my children [the fifth is a toddler] have received Christ, and my husband returned home and also invited the Lord into his heart. I appreciate the counseling I still get from the Women's Division."

Women shackled by both alcohol and narcotics stumble up the stairway to the Women's Division as a place of last resort for help. "Helen" couldn't stumble up the stairway, however— she had to be helped. For during a lost weekend making a round of taverns on West Madison Street, she met with an accident and was taken to Cook County Hospital, her leg broken. The social service department of the hospital later referred her to the Mission.

"That was OK with me," she later said. "I was sick from the lack of narcotics. Besides, I wanted to see what kind of racket they had. What impressed me, though, was that everyone was so happy and laughing. I thought, 'If I could only feel like they look!'

"I went to a meeting that night. I thought they didn't know what they were talking about, having never been hustlers, drunks, or junkies. Next morning I didn't leave and nobody asked me to. I worked, helping with the dishes, all the time seeing peace and happiness around me. That's what I wanted.

"At the meeting that night when they asked if I wanted the Lord to forgive me, I still said no. Saturday I got new clothes and that night at the meeting I burst into tears. I wanted so terribly to be decent—to have peace.

"Elaine took me to the prayer room where we talked for hours. I told her that if I had to stop drinking, life would be impossible. She said that the Lord would help me stop. Suddenly I felt strong and got down on my knees and asked the Lord to save me from my sins. I said, 'Lord, You've heard what You have to work with. If there is anything here You can use, I am Yours.'

"I felt like I was scrubbed inside when I got off my knees. The wonder of it all, even after all these years. It was January 11 that I was converted. January 11 is my birthday."

One of the most unusual cases ever to come to the Women's Division was Mary Howell, sent by a social worker when a judge released her from Women's Court in Chicago. She learned to drink in New York City, then after going to Kansas City began to hop from job to job as well as tavern to tavern. Later, living in a little room over a saloon in St. Louis, she fell victim to delirium tremens. A voice seemed to say: "Mary, get down and pray." She got on her knees beside her bed. But then the voice directed to get on the other side. She got on the other side, and now the voice was directing her to change sides again. Around and around the room she went, until she looked out the window and thought she saw her boyfriend, Frank, hanging from a telephone pole.

Finally, Mary called the police and ended up in a psychopathic hospital. Some time later she made her way to Chicago. It was the year 1930 and the Skid Row population was larger than ever because of the Depression. Here began a pattern of living death that went on almost unchanged for 27 years! Again and again Mary Howell was in and out of Women's Court and Women's Prison at the Bridewell. Later, it was the standard thing to take her to the County Psychopathic Hospital and finally to the State Hospital, either at Kankakee or Manteno.

When Mary arrived at the Mission in 1957, things happened swiftly. She tells it in these words:

"I got a bath and clean clothes, and Elaine Chobanoff prayed with me following the evening service. I confessed Jesus Christ as my personal Lord and Saviour, even though my mind was still confused. During the night, Elaine read Scripture to me.

I had ugly thoughts: It seemed that Elaine was planning to kill me. Yet, somehow, as she read the Bible almost the night through, the words began to make sense to me. I can't be sure what she read but sometime during the night she probably read this verse from John 4 which has become so true in my life, 'Whosoever drinketh of the water that I shall give him shall never thirst.' I'm so glad that I drank of the water that Christ gives."

Today, if you should visit Pacific Garden Mission on a Saturday night and attend the testimony service, the soloist just might be a small, dainty woman of about 60—Mary Howell. Because of her love for the Old Lighthouse and her desire to communicate the gospel to others, she sings with all her heart. You wouldn't rank her with the better voices of our day, but if you knew her story, you'd think her singing as sweet as that of a nightingale. Is it any wonder that Mary Howell and thousands of other women thank God for the day they came to the Women's Division, a haven in a big city?

Chapter 14

WELCOME, GI!

IN THE SUMMER of 1942 the U.S. and its allies were finding the going extremely rough. German submarines and bombers sank 22 of 33 ships, including 15 American ones, in a convoy in July. In the Pacific the U.S. and Japanese navies swung wildly at each other, the U.S. gaining an advantage in winning the Battle of Midway in June but reeling back when the Japanese invaded Guadalcanal in August. Young men in growing numbers were being inducted into the armed forces to strengthen the American military program.

That same summer, in Oklahoma City, Oklahoma, for special meetings, Harry Saulnier spotted a war-related news item that quickened his pulse:

"The U.S. Army will take over the Stevens Hotel, the world's largest, and the Congress Hotel on August 1 to house members of the air forces. . . . The Stevens Hotel, which has 3000 rooms, is expected to house between 9,000 and 10,000 men. The Congress has 900 rooms and will accommodate about 5,000 men."

Laying aside the newspaper, Saulnier exclaimed, "This is it!" Anyone who happened to hear him may have wondered what he meant but not the Lord. God knew all about what had been going on in the mind of the big Frenchman who in his two years at the helm of the Pacific Garden Mission had already shown that he could not be content with the status quo. For months the streets of downtown Chicago had been dotted in increasing numbers by young men and women in khaki and blue. Ever since the Lord had given the Mission two additional buildings, it was a growing desire on the part of Saulnier and the staff to minister to this transient, spiritually needy crop of war-bound Americans. A few blocks away the USO Center swarmed with GI's; PGM would, by God's grace and the aid of His people, open a *Christian* Servicemen's Center! With the Army-commandeered hotels only two blocks away, the challenge was more colossal than ever.

Saulnier rushed back to Chicago to set machinery in action. On November 29, Claudus M. McDaniel, director of the Center, opened the doors and welcomed the first GI's. Here they could unwind while playing ping-pong or shuffleboard in the recreation room, or they could write home or just relax while reading wholesome books and the latest Christian magazines in the library at one end of the chapel. Always available, as today, were refreshments in the Canteen with its Western motif. But best of all, friendly, fatherly personal workers were there to show the GI's how to enlist in the Lord's army.

In the first two months nearly 5000 soldiers, sailors, marines, and coastguardsmen, including women in the various branches, crossed the threshold of the new Center. And in many homes across the land Christian parents rejoiced as unsaved sons and daughters placed their trust in Jesus Christ in answer to prayer. All told, some 100 GI's professed Christ in the first two months, and many others were restored to fellowship with God. Two hundred and fifty New Testaments, supplied by the Gideons, the Chicago Bible Society, and the Moody Bible Institute Colportage, were distributed, along with 20,000 pieces of gospel literature given to GI's on the street and in nearby train depots, as well as in the Center.

The guest register at the Center looked like a worldwide directory of American army and navy bases. Men from Hawaii, Australia, New Zealand, and Canada signed the book. GI's in increasing numbers found their way to the Center from Chicago area stations like the Stevens and Congress Hotels, Navy Pier, and Great Lakes Naval Training Station. Because of the spiritual tone of the Center and the fact that war is a serious matter,

GI's unhesitatingly opened up and talked to counselors about problems.

Among the godly counselors in those early days of the Center were C. E. Bulander, head of the personal work corps, Mrs. Bulander, Edward Ockert, C. E. Davis, and John Baergen. Many Christian laymen and students from Christian schools in Chicagoland came to assist, along with faithful groups of women from area churches (as today) who prepared refreshments in the Canteen from 9:00 A.M. to midnight. In homes and churches hundreds were backing the ministry with fervent prayer.

On December 15, 1942, two weeks after the official opening of the Center, joy filled the hearts of the PGM staff as the final payment of the 30,000 dollar mortgage was made on the buildings housing the Center. Retiring the mortgage reduced the Mission endowment fund to a small amount. Established by gifts from Mother Clarke, Billy Sunday, and others, the fund was used to help pay for the Mission building as well as the buildings housing the Center.

By the spring of 1943, with the Allies sending the war into high gear, GI's in greater numbers were finding salvation. The report was: " 'The fields are already white unto harvest.' Opportunities are limitless for personal soul-winning. The boys are eager to hear the Word. Face to face with danger and death, they are concerned about their souls."

In the month of March 398 decisions were recorded, and the number soared to more than 800 in April and 764 in May. Among these was a Canadian in Scottish Highland kilts who knelt in the Canteen kitchen and received Christ. Another was an Indian boy just graduated from a Chicago training school. After accepting Christ he handed the personal worker an unopened whiskey bottle, signifying his clean break with Satan and the world.

A sailor named Milo was typical of many of the GI's stationed at Chicagoland installations. He told his story in these terms:

"I got my first liberty on a Saturday night. Chicago was a

new town to me. My buddies had been sent to another school, so I was alone in a strange city. A gang of fellows from Navy Pier took me with them and we headed for the Loop. I felt like celebrating—it was a long time between liberties. I ended in a bar on South State. I knew that liquor was the devil's instrument, but I couldn't stop using it, although it didn't satisfy.

"I went walking down South State, wondering how to spend the rest of the evening. At the Servicemen's Center the doorman invited me in. The folks in there had something I wanted. I was convicted that night, but I wasn't ready to trade sin for salvation. However, the Lord never let me rest until I surrendered. Sunday I went with the gang again, but there was no joy for me. I started back to the Pier early. God guided my steps to the Center. I went in tired of my load of sin and longing for peace of heart. Christ cleansed my heart that night, and as the burden of sin rolled away unspeakable peace came into my life. I returned to the base a saved and happy man. I had done nothing. Jesus Christ paid it all on Calvary!"

Interestingly, Carl, a friend of Milo's, also found his way to the Center and came to Christ, unknown to Milo.

When he came to the Stevens Hotel, Carl found a real stamping ground on nearby South State. Everything he naturally looked for he found there—places to drink and gamble. Winning—or losing—a week's army pay in an evening was nothing to Carl. After a drinking party one night, he was walking down the street with a girl he had picked up. In front of the Servicemen's Center the doorman invited them in. Carl completed his story:

"We were drinking coffee in the Canteen—we needed it badly—when Mr. Davis approached our table and led the conversation to things of the Lord. John 3:16 reached my heart, but the gospel only served to harden the girl with me. As soon as I decided for the Lord, she said, 'You're too religious.' And that was that. The poor girl is still roaming State Street looking for servicemen. In February—about two weeks after I was

saved—I ran into my old drinking partner, Milo. The first thing
he said was 'I'm saved now!'

"'So am I,' I said, 'Praise the Lord!'"

Carl summed up the fellowship at the Center with this comment: "Since I have been living with the Lord Jesus Christ as
my Saviour, I can say with the other boys at the Center that
every day is sweeter than the day before. Christian fellowship
at the Center is precious, and I have made many real friends."

As news of the busy Servicemen's Center spread to Christians,
gifts increased to keep the door wide open. Sunday School
classes, young people's societies, and Daily Vacation Bible
Schools sent in money. One gift came from a Sunday school
class started by Chaplain T. H. Makin, who had visited PGM
while on duty at Great Lakes. Another gift was mailed from
Camp Roberts, California, with this note from Chicago area
resident Pvt. Lloyd Cory: "They had a table tennis tournament,
hampered by drunks bumping into the table and the contestants,
and I won. They gave me $5 for my efforts. I'm turning it over
to be used as God directs for the Center. I wish they had something like that near here. Thank God that He's still in the soul-
saving business."

Some of the gifts were used to increase the efficiency of the
Center, as a completely equipped dormitory with some 50 cots
were added in the spring of 1944. Until then some GI's slept on
sofas in the Center, and others, with insufficient money to rent
a hotel room, were staying all night in nightclubs and theaters
or walking the streets. In the first year, 6500 GI's spent the
night in the new dormitory, and more than 800 of these made
professions of faith in Christ.

As the Allies gained momentum in both theaters of operation
in late 1944, thousands of GI's, including women in uniform
who found a welcome overnight in the Women's Division, had
visited the Center and hundreds had made professions of faith
in the Saviour. Follow-up letters went out to all of them, and
cards and letters were mailed to the homes of GI's who signed

the register. Naturally, hearts were warmed in homes almost around the world wherever Allied servicemen lived.

Typical of some of the thank-you letters from Christian parents was this one from a Michigan mother: "I didn't know until I had read what you wrote that my son had accepted Christ as his Saviour. I wrote him at once and told him how I rejoiced on knowing about it and that it was the most wonderful gift a mother could possibly have for Christmas. He went into service when he was eighteen, two years ago this February. He expects to be going overseas anytime now. It means everything to me to know he has Jesus with him."

A Tennessee woman wrote of her joy upon hearing from her husband that he had come to Christ in the Center. "He wrote me all about it," she stated, "and said you all had made him happier than he had been since he left home, and he knew now he didn't have a thing to worry about."

A letter from Mrs. David E. Schiesser, of Weehawken, New Jersey, brought both sad and glad news. Her oldest son, Edward, found Christ at the Old Lighthouse and was promoted to heaven three years later. Going through his personal effects, the grief-stricken mother found a gospel tract that he had picked up at PGM. Then it was that she understood the change that had come into his life. Until then Mrs. Schiesser had been speculating into matters of religion and had embraced the Old Testament centered teachings of Seventh-Day Adventism. She wrote: "Edward was only twenty years old June 30, 1943, when he went home to heaven. I know he is waiting on the other shore for me, his mother, who found the tract he got in Chicago in 1940 and thereby was able to shake off the grave clothes of Moses' time and to emerge into the light of the true 'Sabbath,' the Lord Jesus Christ, in whom I find my rest, praise His precious name."

By the time the war ended in 1945, the Servicemen's Center had in nearly three years welcomed more than 450,000 GI's, and personal workers had recorded some 16,000 decisions for

Christ. With the formal closing of the USO Center in 1946, the PGM Center remained wide open, offering servicemen food, overnight accommodations, and recreation—and, best of all, the gospel.* It proved a wise decision, for in peacetime years there has been a continuous stream of men in uniform visiting the Center. In the first five years after the war an annual average of 50,000 men signed in and 5500 professed Christ. During the 1950's, 26,000 servicemen came each year and professions of faith averaged 4500. In the 1960's, the annual averages have been 17,000 visitors and 4000 professions. (Percentages of men making professions of faith have been higher in peacetime simply because personal workers are able to counsel more thoroughly with more men when the Canteen is not crowded.) All told, the Center has hosted over a million GI's and has recorded 108,000 decisions for Christ.

The Korean War, bringing a sharp increase in the draft, swelled the numbers visiting the Center. Some years ago a Japanese major professed Christ during a stay, and more recently a young Ethiopian flier training at Chanute Air Force Base, Illinois, responded to the gospel.

During the war years and in the months immediately following personal workers saw the effects of war upon the minds and bodies of some of the fellows. In 1946 a discharged sailor suddenly became white and broke into sobs as a worker dealt with him. "They kept on coming, coming, coming!" the young man exclaimed. "We couldn't do a thing, for our guns were washed overboard. So they just kept driving at us. There was screaming, and blood ran over the deck, as they kept on coming. Finally, we had orders to leave the ship and leave our wounded buddies behind—many of whom were dying."

The worker tried to calm this ex-sailor as he relived his experience in the battle of Okinawa. Upon hearing of Christ's

---

*The USO Center was reopened on a smaller scale Christmas 1950. The only other Chicago center is Victory Center, operated by the Christian Business Men's Committee of Chicago. The PGM unit is the only fully equipped Center with a dormitory and open around the clock.

never-failing sufficiency, the fellow opened wide his heart's door and received the Saviour. When he left the Center, he left in God's perfect peace.

The cases of Careaga and Leirmo, GI buddies who came to the Center in 1948, caused much rejoicing among the Mission staff. Sgt. Rudy Careaga came to the Center with a tale of woe. He had come to Chicago to have a good time. Then there was a girl, liquor, and knockout drops—and his money disappeared. A personal worker, Charles Lee Hayes, listened to Careaga's story and offered his sympathy, then proceeded to help Careaga see that his problem had resulted from the sin that ruled his life. Under the mighty power of the Holy Spirit, his heart was melted and a desire to be saved manifested itself. Before he left the Center, he actually was glad he had been robbed, for through the experience he found the Lord Jesus Christ as his personal Saviour.

But that was not the end of contact with Careaga. Next day he returned with another soldier, S. Sgt. Thomas Leirmo, who also had been sampling Satan's dainties in South State Street establishments. Personal worker Hayes dealt with Leirmo about his soul but got the brush off. Next day he spent part of the day taking the two GI's swimming, after buying a pair of swimming trunks for Leirmo. Afterward, the two GI's went on their way to take temporary jobs in a Chicago restaurant until their furloughs were up. Hayes' heart ached for Thomas Leirmo as he prayed for him. He had such a need for Christ, yet the little talk Hayes had had with him seemed to have had no effect.

Then one day about three weeks later, Leirmo dropped into the Canteen to see Hayes. "Hey there," he said, his face beaming. "Remember me? I want to pay back what I owe you for the swimming trunks." Hayes pulled himself up to full height and looked him square in the eye. "Sarge, I'm not interested in the money—I gave you the trunks. I'm interested in knowing how you stand with the Lord."

Leirmo beamed and told a story that thrilled Hayes. "I'm

all right with the Lord. I finally came to the conclusion that there was something lacking in my life. I believed that the Christians at the Servicemen's Center had this 'something.' Then I realized my need for Christ. So one evening, not long after you talked with me, I knelt down in my hotel room and accepted Christ as my Saviour. Until then I had always believed that religion was a theory that no one could prove, but now I know better. No one but the Lord Jesus Christ will ever realize how much my life has been changed. Although I am still in the Army with duties to perform, the inner change—the awakening of my long lost soul—is my cause for rejoicing."

A Richmond, Virginia, boy David Y. Apt visited the Center in 1950 and made a profession of faith in Christ before he shipped out for duty in the Korean War. A few months later his mother, Mrs. David Apt, wrote: "He was sent over to Japan and on to Korea, where he was killed November 21. The letter you sent here to him has been more precious to me than anything I have! After going on to Japan he wrote . . . he was reading his Bible every chance he had. He was killed in action instantly."

Dean Ford, a sailor who came to the Old Lighthouse in 1954, has often thanked God for the strategic placement of the Center. As a 15-year-old he had come into a personal relationship with Jesus Christ but began drifting in the Navy. One day on pass from Great Lakes, he reluctantly joined other sailors in a tour of South State Street's burlesque houses, tattoo parlors, and saloons. Dean didn't like what he saw—until he looked up and saw the big PGM sign, "JESUS SAVES." The doorman invited Dean and his friends in, but only Dean went inside. The others scoffed and left. In the Canteen the young sailor came back to Christ, broken before God and confessing his condition. That night he stayed overnight in the dormitory, rejoicing that he was back in the fold.

In the months that followed, Dean Ford was a regular visitor at the Old Lighthouse. He made many friends. When he was ready to be transferred, he talked one evening with a little man who has now gone to be with the Lord. It was Dan Kearney, onetime Irish song-and-dance man and drunkard who had come out of a mental institution to receive Christ at the Mission and become a new man in Him.

"There are two kinds of tracts in these packages, Dean," he said, giving him the bundles. "There's a lot of meat to both of them. I hope you'll use them often."

Dean told Dan he had no idea where he would use them. But Dean passed them out to other GI's and ordered more and more. Later, he married. Today he and his wife, Wilma, serve the Lord as missionaries under the West Indies Mission in the jungles of Surinam, South America.

Over the years, many GI's and ex-servicemen have returned to the Old Lighthouse with a word of thanks for the spiritual counseling they got, another indication that the ministry bears lasting fruit.

Bob Kelly of Cleveland, Ohio, dropped in one day in 1950 to say thanks to Coach Ed Ockert for pointing him to the Lamb of God three years before. "At the time I didn't understand what was happening, but now I realize I was being born again," he testified. "It has been my privilege to bring a few others to Christ also."

Ockert, incidentally, proved himself one of the Center's most able and colorful personal workers in the 20 years he served. Joining the staff in 1944 when he quit athletic coaching at 70 years of age, he worked tirelessly. Boys were drawn to him as a man. Almost till his death on March 20, 1964, at 89 he bounced about, playing table tennis and shuffleboard with visiting servicemen. But always he sat down with the fellows, Bible in hand, and with a gnarled finger showed them verses relating to salvation. In 1957 Ockert revealed to a close friend that up to June of that year he had been used of God to lead 16,620 boys to Christ. This number, of course, was greatly increased during the next seven years until his death. He won his last soul to Christ at the Center on February 28, 1964, became ill soon afterward, and never was able to return to his job.

Today other faithful personal workers greet and work with the men in uniform in the same tradition of Ockert. Gus Magnuson, an elderly Swede, has been on the staff since 1955. Other workers include Peter Potkonjak, a retired leather worker from Marshall Field's who began working in the Center in 1943; John Nordstrom, former telephone company employee who has been winning GI's since 1950; and John Tichy, ex-missionary to Alaska who has served at the Mission since 1955.

Thus, today the door remains wide open to the man in uniform. Since the military buildup in 1965 in connection with the Viet Nam conflict, the Center is buzzing with increased activity. The message for the GI, however, is the same as in the early days of the Center: "Ye must be born again" (John 3:7).

Chapter 15

FILMING THE PGM STORY

"DEAD!" The house detective examined the dead woman's body for evidences of murder or suicide and then summoned the coroner.

"Yes, it looks like murder, Tom." That was all. Evelyn's death was the climax of a brief but horrible existence consisting of a continual round of brothels, police courts, dope dens, and street walking.

Born in a small Western town, of good parents, the girl had had the normal childhood allotted to every red-blooded American. There were days of horseback riding, games, and playing dolls. And then high school.

"Mother, I've a job at Pop Johnson's soda fountain!" Evelyn, breathless with excitement, announced one evening as she tossed her books on the sofa. "I get 75 cents an hour, and work five days a week." Thrilled at the new independence of making some money of her own, she worked hard for three months. In those prewar days, a schoolgirl could buy a lot of things from her earnings of 75 cents an hour.

One afternoon a stranger entered the ice cream store and ordered a Coke. He watched the girl as she filled her orders, and a satisfied smile lurked in his eyes.

"How old are you, miss?"

"Sixteen, sir, my last birthday."

"You're too beautiful to be stuck to this job. I can help you make big money. Hundreds of dollars a week. Easy. Interested?" He waited, allowing the suggestion of wealth and luxury to take its effect. It was so simple. It always was.

That was the beginning. First prostitution. Then drugs to stifle the conscience. Next, the police court. But one day she heard the voice of Him who said, "I am the light of the world: he that followeth me shall not walk in darkness, but shall have the light of life." And at the Pacific Garden Mission another Samaritan woman found Christ as her Saviour.

And this is why she died. When the man who first enticed her came back into her life, she could give but one answer. "I'm not my own. I'm bought with a price—the blood of Jesus Christ. I can no longer have anything to do with you!"

And so he killed her. Murder? Yes, but a better word is *martyrdom!*

This story, from the May 1945 *Pacific Garden Mission News,* set the creative gears of the mind of Superintendent Saulnier into action once again. For years he had been talking to various ones about putting the PGM story on film to show God's hand in action through the outreach of the Mission. Such a film, Saulnier reasoned, could, if expertly done, arouse slumbering church people to the need for harvesting souls right in their own backyards and at the same time be an evangelistic tool to be used by the Holy Spirit to convict the unsaved and bring them to Christ. The story of Evelyn could easily become part of that film.

In 1948 a new filming company, Cavalcade Productions, operated by Christian men, invaded the Mission with cameras and other motion-picture equipment. By this time Evelyn's story had been combined with other stories in a script that touched on several phases of the Mission ministry. And for many weeks parts of the Mission and places along Skid Row became a film set. In those days the unexpected was the expected.

For example, Loiell Hyler, assistant superintendent and one of the Mission's soul winners of that day, made a forced landing on the seat of his baggy trousers on the sidewalk in front of a South State Street tavern from which he had been ungraciously shoved by a burly tavern employee.

At first glance someone may have concluded that Hyler had backslidden and was a candidate for Mission aid. But in hitting Skid Row with the seat of his pants, Hyler was very much still working for the Lord; for a Cavalcade cameraman that day was carefully recording the incident. Hyler was cast as Bill Jennings, a business executive whom alcohol had ruined. In a later scene in the film Jennings would visit the Mission and drink of the Water of Life and find freedom from his habit and a wonderful new life walking with Jesus Christ.

The film, *Out of the Night,* had its premier showing on the evening of October 15, 1948, in Chicago's Moody Memorial Church. Since that day there have been well over 4000 individual showings of this 30-minute film before an estimated 700,000 viewers. In addition, the film has been shown on several TV stations, increasing the number of viewers into the millions.

Encouraged by the response to *Out of the Night,* Saulnier and the PGM Board authorized another film, *The Street.* It was released to churches, prison missionaries, and others in March 1953. Also a documentary in sound and color, *The Street* dramatizes the story of a young man in a small town who drifts into crime and flees to Skid Row. Here he hides out, visiting taverns until his money is gone. He sleeps in alleys, and frostbite sends him to the PGM Clinic. Here a godly doctor leads him to Christ. Harry Saulnier counsels him and advises him to retrace his crooked way and surrender himself for his crimes. The superintendent accompanies him to his hometown where an understanding judge places him on probation in Saulnier's custody.

The Street, like the first film, has been used widely. Through more than 3000 showings, more than 520,000 have seen this 35-minute glimpse into the Mission ministry.

The Mission has circulated 181 copies of *Out of the Night* and 86 copies of *The Street,* and more than 70 copies of both films have been purchased by outside agencies for evangelistic purposes.

Most showings have been in Sunday evening or midweek services in churches, but some of the most fruitful showings have been in jails, prisons, and military camps and installations.

In addition to the two movies, the Mission in 1960 produced *The Cross Roads,* a color slide and filmstrip closeup look at the Mission in action. This production is available on a freewill offering basis, whereas the motion pictures are normally rented.

No attempt has been made at the Mission to record the results seen from these films, but the harvests have been substantial. Where there haven't been actual conversions, the Holy Spirit has shown young people the pitfalls of sin and stirred many lethargic church members to prayer and action concerning ministering the gospel to Skid Row people not only in Chicago but in their own cities.

Results of the film ministry are reflected in the letters of those who have used the films:

The chaplain of a state training school for boys reported that he showed *The Street* to 150 inmates, and fifteen boys raised their hands to indicate that they were making decisions for Christ.

A Minnesota pastor reported that a businessman about 30 years of age, a father of four children, had come to Christ through a showing of *The Street.*

A report from Idaho indicated that "the Spirit was pleased to move twenty-eight young people . . . to make first-time decisions for Jesus Christ" after they viewed *The Street.*

A West Virginia man showed *Out of the Night* in five churches and in a jail and wrote that "we had two converts at the jail and seventy-nine dedications to the Lord as a result of seeing the picture."

In South Carolina a church used *Out of the Night* to encourage young people to abstain from the use of alcoholic beverages, and some 150 responded to a pledge of abstinence.

Countless pastors and others have reported that church people have for the first time become burdened for the souls of those leading a Skid Row existence.

Now and then there is written into the record of the Old Lighthouse a dramatic account of someone who has come to the Saviour through one of the films. The George Guttrich story is a case in point. His story climaxes in a way that clearly shows the value of the film ministry.

Guttrich grew up on a farm in the sand country of Jasper County, Indiana. Following high school and business school, he married and settled in Chicago. Here the country boy began to live (or so he thought) as he worked directly with the vice-president in charge of a distillery his firm operated as a sideline. Guttrich carried the keys to the sample liquor cabinet of the firm, drinking all he wanted at no cost to him. Part of his job was to entertain prospective customers.

Fortunately, George Guttrich held his own with liquor, finding that black coffee would fix him for a productive working day. But nonetheless he had the habit; and when the company sold the distillery, he began buying his own liquor—a bottle a week—usually for Saturday nights.

Thus, sometimes he had a throbbing head when he sent his son, Gordie, on Sunday mornings to meet an elderly neighbor, a Mrs. Cornett who took him to Sunday school in a little church across the alley.

Faithful Mrs. Cornett invited the Guttriches, who considered themselves average Chicagoans, to the little church, but they went only on special occasions. For example, George Guttrich sat in the little church one Easter feeling like an outsider. He couldn't sing with conviction the songs these godly people sang so lustily. Neither could he smile the way a man named Walter Mishler did when he shook George's hand that morning.

He compared his sour-looking face with Mishler's. Here he was, so tense and full of fear that he wasn't even driving his car except when he had to. *I need what these warm, contented people have,* Guttrich reasoned. *But what do they have? And how do I get it?*

One night in the summer of 1948 nine-year-old Gordie came home from church and walked straight into Dad's room.

"I just gave my life to Jesus Christ, Daddy."

"This really pulled at my heart, and all through the fall months I felt that pull," recalls Guttrich. "I began attending the little church. And one night, on Gordie's invitation, I went to see what he termed 'a swell movie' called *Out of the Night.* As the picture went on, I noticed a little ten-year-old girl wipe away a tear. I only half saw the picture, but in it I felt more than understood the transforming power of Jesus Christ! When it was over, in the silence of my own empty soul, I knelt with the ten-year-old girl at the altar and asked Jesus Christ to cleanse my heart. When I got up, I could not only smile like Walter Mishler, but I went right home and took my wife, Edith, for a ride in the car! The fear neurosis was gone along with my old life. And it's never come back."

George Guttrich's exciting walk with Jesus Christ resulted in his wife's stepping fully into God's kingdom. Thus, as Guttrich himself said in an "Unshackled!" story, "We no longer qualified as an average Chicago family.   Unfortunately, God doesn't have any place in the *average* home of today as He now has in ours."

Norma Lawecki of Toledo, Ohio, was the "girl with a heart of stone," according to Mission records, until she saw *Out of the Night.* With an unhappy childhood, part of it spent in a children's home, she became especially rebellious after her mother found Christ as her Saviour and urged Norma to go to church with her. Two times Norma went to the altar and *said* that she wanted Christ, but her life remained unchanged.

Finally she quit church, despite her mom's pleas to go with her, and for about 15 years tried to find satisfaction in pleasure. A physical breakdown in 1950 hospitalized her on two occasions. By this time she lived away from home, a girl as thin as a sapling and a constant smoker. Occasionally Mother would call and beg her to go to church with her, and Norma would play the same record: "No. And how many times do I have to say it? I work all week and Sunday is the only time I have to work at home!"

But then one day Mother called and bubbled: "It's a motion picture. I want you to see at the church. It starts at 7:30."

"I can't make it by then," Norma replied.

"By 8?"

"Well, OK, but it'll probably be half over."

"I'll pray that Harry Saulnier is late getting here from Chicago!" Norma's mother chuckled.

Because of bad driving conditions, so he announced, Saulnier didn't arrive with the film until 8:00. Thus, Norma was there in good time. As the film was shown, she sat as if in a trance. At the close of the picture, she fell to her knees and wept. A woman prayed with her and talked to her about Jesus Christ. Norma told her she had already tried twice to be a Christian, but that didn't stop the personal worker. And soon Norma began to see her trouble: "You mean if I mean business with Christ this time, He'll receive me?"

In her "Unshackled!" story, Norma Lawecki said:

"I found out as I reached out for Him in faith. I became His and He poured out His love on me, washing away all the hate and evil thoughts that had once controlled my mind. Soon He told me to stop leaning on cigarettes, to depend on Him and His grace. And somehow, until I obeyed Him, He didn't have me. Though there have been times when I've disappointed Him, God has done everything He could for me. I didn't have anything before I knew Him. Now I have a home—not a fancy one, but it's ours. He gave me real friends that pray for me— not the fair-weather kind. I can't describe the depression and darkness I knew before I was saved. I didn't want to live but was afraid to die. God has taken all that away. Truly, He made Ezekiel 11:19 come true in my life: 'I will take the stony heart out of their flesh, and will give them an heart of flesh.' "

Is it any wonder, with stories such as these, that the staff of the Old Lighthouse rejoice in the fact that the Mission heeded God's call in 1948 to communicate the life-changing gospel through reels of movie film?

Chapter 16

DRAMA ON THE AIRWAVES

NEVER CONTENT to minister the gospel only to those who wander into the Old Lighthouse, Harry Saulnier in the early years of his tenure talked to the Lord on many occasions about a radio outreach. As the staff grew, he talked with them about the advantages of a Mission broadcast and got many to pray with him. Somehow, sometime, he told associates, God was going to show how the Mission could share by radio the gospel and the way it can change lives.

In the early months of 1945 it appeared that his prayer was being answered. Saulnier sold radio station WAIT, Chicago, on giving the Mission an early-morning 15-minute program. On many occasions he worked at the Mission till the early morning hours, then rushed home for a few hours sleep before arising at 5:30 A.M. to come back into the Loop to be in the radio studio by 7:30. The program, called "Doorway to Heaven," went on at 7:45. Saulnier earnestly presented the gospel and related stories of changed lives at the Mission. Converts themselves often came to tell personally of the transformation Christ had wrought in their lives. Things were going well until three months later when WAIT changed its policy and dropped all religious broadcasting.

Similar programs followed on stations WGES on Chicago's West Side and WMBI, the Moody Bible Institute station. As fine as they were, the programs were only local, and always Saulnier had the feeling that God had greater things ahead for the Mission in the field of radio.

One day in the late 1940's, a conversation with an advertis-

137

ing man sent Saulnier's mind racing in another direction. "Why not dramatize stories of Mission converts like other stories you often hear on the radio?" the ad man suggested. "Make the stories live. Tremendous things have happened in the lives of many of the converts. Dramatize their life stories and you'll appeal to all sorts of people. Perhaps a big company would be willing to sponsor such a program."

Saulnier liked the idea, but he felt it would be impractical to tie in with a sponsor. God's people would underwrite and pay for the broadcast, assuring the Mission of complete control of program content.

The board of trustees voted to move ahead, and Saulnier hired John Gillies, experienced radioman formerly with WMBI, to prepare a 15-minute pilot program. This was presented at the Mission in July 1950. Gillies got a green light to proceed with a half hour script on Billy Sunday, to begin a regular weekly series. John Camp, radio advertising executive, took over the account and arranged for a weekly broadcast at 11 P.M. on Saturdays on powerful, clear-channel WGN. Now the Mission would reach into homes for hundreds of miles across mid-America.

Many names were suggested for the new program, but Saulnier, a man not easily pleased with titles, remained unmoved by them all. On a visit to WGN, Camp mentioned the problem of finding a suitable name. An ex-navy man, sensing the need for a short, descriptive title, suddenly remembered his days aboard ship. "In beginning a radio call, we'd begin by saying shackled and end with unshackled. How about 'Unshackled' for a title?"

Hearing the name, Harry Saulnier straightened and his face brightened, as a man suddenly awakening from a trance. "That's it! It's different and yet it suggests just what we want the program itself to say: that Christ can break the fetters of sin and set the sinner free!"

With John Gillies directing and Lucille Becker at the organ

to provide mood music between scenes, "Unshackled!" got under way officially on September 23, 1950, as a cast of radio dramatists, scripts in hand, gathered in a WGN studio to recreate the life and conversion of Billy Sunday.

Though the program got off to a good start, John Gillies soon resigned. Meantime God had been working in the life of a young woman well known in secular radio circles:

At 33 years of age, Eugenia Price headed up a successful radio production office that turned out scripts for such popular shows as "In Care of Aggie Horn," "Joyce Jordan, M.D.," and "First Nighter." But now, after 10 years in the big time, she was wondering what success had really gotten her. Here she was with the things that money would buy, but she was bored. Finally she called up a childhood chum Ellen Riley, the girl who had played the piano in young people's. Ellen had made Jesus Christ the center of her life and was now serving Him in full-time work in New York City. Ellen spent a week's vacation with Genie and shared Christ with her. But Genie held out until late September 1949, when she flew to New York and decided to have it out with Ellen.

There, in a hotel room on October 2, after a long spiritual struggle, Genie Price caught hold of Ellen's arm and whispered, "OK, honey, you're right. I want all of Him." In that dramatic moment Genie opened her heart and invited Christ to take over.

A year later God had put her in touch with Pacific Garden Mission. And on the first Saturday night in October 1950 Genie Price, who had grown rapidly in the Christian life, was using her radio talents for God, directing "Unshackled!" as it invaded homes and automobiles of late-night listeners in Chicago and suburbs and out across the rolling farmlands of the great Midwest.

While professional radio people were hailing the program as a religious broadcast with distinct quality, the Holy Spirit was moving upon hearts of listeners. As the weeks passed, the mail volume grew. Some letters had contributions in them—

vital to the continuation of the broadcast. But most gratifying were those who indicated that they had heard God's voice. One man brought back to the Lord through "Unshackled!" sang with the converts' chorus during the 73rd PGM anniversary rally a few weeks after the broadcast was begun.

By early 1952 Harry Saulnier could see God's hand working out the details to beam the program to a wider area. In addition to a more choice hour on WGN—7:30 P.M.—a dozen other radio stations were airing the program each week, including WHAI, Greenfield, Massachussetts; WFHG, Bristol, Virginia; WREX, Duluth, Minnesota; and KUOA, Siloam Springs, Arkansas. In later years, Saulnier has seen the network grow to some 230 stations in U.S. and 12 foreign countries on six continents—North America, South America, Africa, Australia, Asia, and Europe. One of the latest stations to begin airing "Unshackled!" is the Trans World Radio outlet at Monte Carlo, Monaco, beaming the gospel to Great Britain and countries of Western Europe. All told, an estimated 10,000,000 people hear "Unshackled!" each week.

In most cases, local stations give time to the Mission as a public service, and the Mission in turn sends the tapes out free of charge. Eleven U.S. broadcasts are sponsored by Christian businessmen, churches, and other groups.

Since 1957, in Chicago radio circles, "Unshackled!" has been treated a lot like some of the drifters whose stories have been told on the broadcast. Whereas WGN welcomed the program in 1950 and recognized it as a popular feature among listeners in years afterward, a policy change in late 1956 kicked "Unshackled!" off the air, and the program landed on WLS in January 1957. In May 1960 WLS changed ownership, and again the Mission broadcast got the cold shoulder as the station decided to do religious broadcasting only on Sundays. Next stop was WCFL, but this too was short-lived as policy changes showed "Unshackled!" the door. Currently, the only Chicago outlet is WMBI-FM on Saturday evenings at 7:00.

All told, the annual budget for "Unshackled!" is 45,000 dollars including actual production and the office expense at the
Mission itself. Because the program seldom stresses a need for
funds, contributions often fail to meet expenses. As a result
more than once the board has talked of the possibility of cutting
back on the radio ministry, but because of the fruits of the work
such suggestions are always tabled.

From the start, it became clear that the broadcast was reaching
alcoholics behind closed doors in city, suburbia, small towns,
and farm homes—doors that were perhaps otherwise closed to
the gospel.

Probably Bill Morrison is the outstanding example of a lis-
tener unshackled from alcoholism. After hearing "Unshackled!"
broadcasts begun in March 1953 by the Christian Business
Men's Committee of Orillia, Ontario, Canada, on radio station
CFOR, Morrison called in a godly pastor and sought help in
coming to the Saviour. In early January 1959 Bill read an
article in *The Montreal Star* that bothered him. He wrote a
letter to the paper giving his story:

> Sir:
>
>   Last week there appeared in your paper an article entitled
> "No Cure for Alcoholism" reporting on statements by Dr.
> David A. Stewart from Toronto.
>
>   I would like to differ with Dr. Stewart, as I myself have
> found the cure. An alcoholic for forty-one years, having con-
> sumed rubbing alcohol, shaving lotion, canned heat, and shoe
> polish for over a period of twenty years, and having fallen
> prey to drug addiction for five years, I one Sunday evening
> heard a radio program from the Pacific Garden Mission en-
> titled "Unshackled!" True-to-life stories were dramatized of
> people whose lives had been reclaimed from alcoholism and
> drug addiction, and the fact occurred to me that what God
> had done for others, He could do for me. I accepted Jesus
> Christ, and surrendered my life to Him. From that day on,
> and for six years now, I have had absolutely no desire for

alcohol or drugs, and the Lord has marvelously undertaken financially and in all other ways, for the needs of myself and my family.

The verse in II Corinthians 5:17, in the Bible, states: "Therefore, if any man be in Christ, he is a new creature: old things are passed away, behold all things are become new." This verse has been proven in my life. I am now on the staff of a rescue mission in this city, and living for the One who has so dramatically changed my life.

BILL MORRISON

Many "Unshackled!" listeners probably are not aware of the fact that Jack Odell, the writer-director of the program since the mid 1950's was himself once an alcoholic and is an indirect convert of the Mission radio ministry. After Air Force duty during World War II, Jack returned to Chicago radio circles, becoming program director of WCFL. But unable to resist whiskey, which had been dogging his career since he moved into radio in the middle 1930's, he lost his job in 1949 and found himself driving a cab.

Finally, his old-time school friend Ward Oury badgered him to meet another radio personality. "Maybe Genie Price, whose radio stories are of real people who found victory over the drink habit, will have some advice for you regarding your problem," Oury suggested.

Jack Odell stalled as long as he could, but one night, at the end of his resources, he consented to meet Miss Price. With understanding, she dealt with him. "You're looking for something, aren't you, Jack?"

"Yeah, I guess I am—a way out."

"There is a way, Jack, through Jesus Christ. He is the Way, and He has a brand new life for you too. It's a gift and you can't have it unless you'll reach out of your own free will and take it. But *when* you take this gift, you'll be free. Can you understand that?"

Jack did understand, and that night as he drove home he

stopped his car, confessed his need, and invited Jesus Christ to be his personal Saviour.

In the months afterward Jack found himself hauling country kids recovering from their first sprees over to Pacific Garden Mission for straightening out. But all the time Jack himself was still struggling with the drink problem, trying to get complete victory. One night in May 1953 Miss Price suggested that Jack attend a Mission service. That night, sitting on the platform facing the Skid Row audience, Jack Odell knew God was dealing with him about the bottle. A few minutes later he got up and gave his testimony, and inside, as he spoke, he sensed that at last his thirst was completely quenched with Living Water.

Soon afterward, Jack Odell took over "Unshackled!" as Genie Price moved on to a program of her own, speaking engagements, and book writing. Like Miss Price, Odell has from the start shown untiring devotion to the program, acutely aware of the far-reaching ministry. He personally interviews story subjects, tracks down leads for colorful dramatizations, and writes scores of letters over the months to obtain authentic information for stories. "Jack's ability is uncanny," says Russ Reed, who has long been associated with Odell and the program as a dramatist. "You have to be with and know Jack to appreciate him. He can do an interview and then turn out a polished script from a few scribbled notes. He has a real grasp of the needs of the program."

Odell may be seen in action on Saturdays from 2:30 to 5:30 P.M. in Boulevard Recording Studio, 632 North Dearborn, in Chicago, as he directs the "Unshackled!" cast in dramatizing stories of Mission converts and others.* Each week up to 100 people, including church groups from distant points, watch the production of the program. After the production of the program many travel two miles south across the business district for a

---

*Plans call for an early move of the production of "Unshackled!" to the Mission itself.

tour of the Mission, a tasty dinner, and then the Saturday evening testimony meeting.

Odell himself serves as announcer for "Unshackled!" as well as script writer and director. From three to six radio artists take parts in a story. And here Christians working the program find opportunity to share Christ with unbelieving artists who appear from time to time. At first, Harry Saulnier hesitated concerning the use of non-Christians. But union regulations required the use of union artists, making it necessary, if the program was to be a quality presentation, to use available talent. As a production was under way one Saturday some years ago, Jack Lester, doing the lead, came over and sat down at the artist's table. "That story is *me!*" he blurted, obviously broken. In the warm spiritual fellowship of Jack Odell, Russ Reed, Harry Elders, and others, Lester crossed over the line and blossomed out as a real believer, and today is going on with the Lord in radio work on the West Coast.

Curiously, some of the conversion stories resulting from "Unshackled!" have themselves been dramatized on the program. Ed and Mary Whitford are today on the foreign field as missionaries because God finally reached Ed through "Unshackled!" Their story was told about six years ago on the program.

Mary had come to Christ one Sunday after Ed had walked out of a church service, taking her with him. She had prayed earnestly for his salvation until one night Ed listened to an "Unshackled!" story. He doesn't remember whose story was told; he only remembers a woman in the story asking, "What are you waiting for? Will there ever be a better time to accept Christ?"

In a moment Mary whispered, "Ed, what are *you* waiting for?"

They were too busy praying to hear the rest of the program. Ed was a new creature with a new-found peace of heart and mind. Inside of a year he felt definitely called to the ministry. He enrolled at Bethel College in St. Paul, Minnesota, and served for a couple of years as pastor of a small church in Wisconsin before leaving for foreign missionary service with Mary.

Glen D. Becker of St. Joseph, Michigan, didn't live to hear his story on "Unshackled!" His granddaughter, Jeanette Becker, wrote the Mission after hearing the story of Ben Engstrom dramatized. Her grandfather was dying of cancer, and she desperately wanted to point him to the Saviour. A booklet, "God's Way of Salvation," was sent to her, and a few days later she reported joyously that "my grandfather just received the Lord . . . and now he's working on Grandmother. In two weeks he's a better Christian than I was in a year." Six weeks later Glen Becker went to be with the Lord.

More and more reports come to the Mission that entire families gather about their radios to hear "Unshackled!" Some report spiritual results. One day in Mendota, Illinois, a young mother sobbed out her heart to God in words like these: "I don't understand what the Bible is all about, but if those people on 'Unshackled!' can get new lives, You must have one for me too. Dear God, forgive me for being mean and cross. Art needs a new wife. The babies need a new mother. Save me or change me—or whatever it is You do for me—right now. In Jesus Christ's name." That was how Mrs. Betty Lou Barker joined her husband, Art, in the Christian walk. Today, with their eight children, they regularly attend a Bible preaching church and make it a habit to listen to "Unshackled!"

A report on "Unshackled!" would not be complete without mention of Joe Carlson, the ex-policeman who spent two years in prison for vote fraud. Out of prison, he served for several years as a watchman and then moved to a better job in a chemical testing laboratory. He retired in 1951 and looked back on a pointless, meaningless life. His mind turned to God, and a fragment from the Bible began flickering through his mind: "Seek ye first the kingdom of God, and his righteousness; and all these things shall be added unto you" (Matt. 6:33). But how did one find the Kingdom of God? Joe Carlson had heard "Unshackled!" several times, so he decided to come to the Mission to find the answer to his question. And so it was that Harry Saulnier pointed Joe Carlson, at the age of 75, to the Saviour. Until his death, he often gave his testimony in Mission meetings.

One of the most unusual instances of a man coming to Christ because of "Unshackled!" was that of a man listed in Mission records as J. P——. Curiously enough, he himself did not hear the broadcast. J. P——'s wife was killed in an automobile accident, sending him into an emotional tailspin. For weeks he went on a drown-my-troubles drinking spree and ended up wandering the streets of Chicago for three days and three nights. He deliberated whether he should commit suicide or seek the help of the police in recovering three suitcases and a radio which had been stolen from him by two men who had dropped him off in Chicago.

At a Chicago police station the desk sergeant was listening to "Unshackled!" when the haggard, penniless J. P—— entered. Hearing his story, the sergeant consoled, "Buddy, we'll call somebody at the Pacific Garden Mission. I'm sure they'll be able to put you up. Not much we can do about the stolen items but we'll be on the look out."

After a good night's rest at the Mission and a morning shave, J. P——, an industrial engineer and a veteran of World War II as well as of the Korean War, found Jesus Christ as Jack Parkes, then assistant superintendent, counseled him. Because friends of the Mission were faithful in providing good used clothing, the Mission was able to provide J. P—— with the necessary clothes. A job was obtained for him in a Chicago hotel.

With "Unshackled!" now beamed to large audiences on six continents, mail averages several hundred pieces a week. Some of the letters bring encouraging news that the original dream of Harry Saulnier and the board members is being fulfilled as the Holy Spirit is tugging at hearts of people in many lands as a result of the broadcast. A Filipino heard "Unshackled!" on station DZAS, Manila. "I have been a liquor addict for ten years," he wrote, "but not since November 1963 when I accidentally listened to the program 'Unshackled!' . . . I totally promise not to drink any single drop of wine, through our Lord Jesus Christ sake [sic]." Letters of counsel went to this man to make sure he had received the new birth.

From South Madras, India, came this comment: "The effect of hearing it stays with me for some time after that program. Every time you close your program with those consoling and soothing words, 'If your life is empty, it can be filled to overflowing,' I want this to happen to me." A follow-up specialist wrote him to help him place his faith in Christ as personal Saviour.

A man who described himself as "a heavy drinker and heavy smoker" in 1963 wrote to the CBMC in Toowoomba, Australia, sponsors of "Unshackled!" on a station there, urging that the program be continued. He said: "Just over twelve months ago it was through a series of these programs that I came to the Lord Jesus Christ. I came to know my sin and that I was in need of a Saviour. Often I suffered from blackouts lasting twenty-four hours or more from excessive drinking. I could find no purpose in life and often my weekly wages were gone in two or three days." This young man was enrolled in a theological college at last report!

Thus, as the late Dr. M. R. De Haan of the Radio Bible Class once put it, "The phenomenal response and acceptance of America's unique radio program, 'Unshackled!' is indeed the work of God. The ministry and outreach of this Lighthouse has been multiplied a thousand times by the open door of radio broadcasting."

Chapter 17

DOCTORING SKID ROW ILLS

IN HIS FIRST YEARS at the Mission Harry Saulnier was well on his way toward earning the title "Doc." While at the Commonwealth Edison Company he had taken a first aid course and had gotten a first aid certificate. So the word got around that the new superintendent had a big bottle of mercurochrome and could bandage a wound with the skill of a medic. As a result, men from the street suffering cuts and bruises incurred in fights or falls came in regularly for repairs.

"In more serious cases we'd stretch them out on one of the tables in the dining hall, bind them up, and send them over to Cook County Hospital," Saulnier recalls.

All of this was better than nothing, but it wasn't good enough. And for that reason the superintendent and the staff prayed for 11 years for professional help.

In 1951 two young medical students from the University of Illinois, Dean Smith and Jack Pollard, strolled into Saulnier's office and announced, "Mr. Saulnier, God has laid it on our hearts to open up a medical clinic here."

"That's an answer to prayer!" Saulnier shot back.

God had been burdening the hearts of members of the Christian Medical Society chapter at the university, they revealed, during the time prayers were going up from the Mission for help in ministering to the aches and pains of Skid Row.

Dr. Dean Smith, now a plastic surgeon in Grand Rapids, Michigan, vividly recalls how God worked out the details of setting up what today is an efficient, modernly-equipped medical clinic serving up to 45 persons a week:

"We were able to generate some enthusiasm among the Christian graduate physicians in the Chicago area who counseled us much. Dr. Gus Hemwall and Dr. John Elsen were some of those who counseled us and guided us. I can remember going with Dr. Hemwall to look over secondhand medical office furniture.

"Another problem was securing the approval of authorities at school. I remember having at least one interview with Dr. Andrew Ivy, then administrative director of the Medical School, and Dr. Stanley Olson, dean. Both of these men were quite warm and friendly and heartily endorsed our activity as long as it was properly supervised.

"As to the beginning of the Clinic itself, it reminded one much of the offering that Israel brought to Moses at the time the Tabernacle was to be built, when the Lord led such as were willing of heart to bring what they had to Him for the Tabernacle. After Mr. Saulnier arranged to have the rooms remodeled for the Clinic use, different members of our Christian Medical Society group contributed things: cabinets, diagnostic equipment, laboratory equipment. Our dental friends from the Dental School even supplied a secondhand dental chair.

"There was no shortage of help. Some of those who helped, besides Jack Pollard, now a radiologist in Boston, were James Peterson, Burton Sutherland, Al Tuftee, Bob Quackenbush, Zerne Chapman, and Del Nelson. When the work was further made known, there were Christian nurses from the various hospitals [members of the Nurses Christian Fellowship] and some nurses who were studying at Moody Bible Institute who came down and helped."

Until 1963 patients trudged up a long stairway to the second floor where the Clinic occupied three relatively small rooms. When the Men's Division and Mission chapel were moved to the old Loyal Hotel building, remodeling began in the original Mission building to provide more Clinic space. Today there's a professional look about the area, consisting of three medical

examining rooms, two dental rooms, an X ray room, quarters
for records and supplies, and a laboratory containing extra supplies and sterilizing equipment. In addition, there's a private
dormitory with four beds where ailing staff personnel may rest.
Eventually it will become a hospital ward when and if round-the-
clock nursing service is available. Currently, a registered nurse
—staff member Audrey Knutson—is on duty from 8:15 A.M.
to 5:15 P.M.

Medical practice at the Clinic is confined largely to most dental problems, first aid, and treatment of minor ailments, including cuts, leg ulcers caused by excessive drinking of wine, colds,
and stomachaches. Those needing more detailed diagnosis and
therapy are referred to the Cook County Hospital or some other
medical treatment center of the city's welfare department. War
veterans, of course, are sent to a Veterans' Administration hospital if special treatment is needed.

Not only Skid Row cases but also mothers and children from
the Women's and Children's Division are treated. They are
examined during the early evening hours. Medical treatment is
given Monday, Wednesday, and Friday evenings, and dental
treatment on Tuesday and Thursday evenings. Christian medical
students continue to make up the main part of the staff, though
a licensed, qualified physician always in attendance guarantees
the Clinic both legal and medical status and guards against
errors in diagnosis and treatment. More than a dozen practicing
physicians and dentists in the area give of their time, coming one
or more times a month.

The evening I visited the Clinic five Northwestern University
students and a physician were on duty, along with four nurses.
A Moody Bible Institute student was there to counsel patients
evidencing spiritual problems.

Some 20 patients, including mothers and children, waited for
a nurse to come and call them to an examining room. I chatted
with several to determine their reason for being at the Clinic:

A pale, gaunt young man from Detroit couldn't shake a cold. He worked on the waterfront and was one minute in a heated building and the next minute outside in the cold.

A white woman waited with her baby, who had diarrhea. The baby appeared to be about 18 months old and had definite Negroid features. The mother said her husband had been in the State Hospital for the past seven years and she was having a difficult time making ends meet. She had three other children.

A pleasant, heavyset man who said he is a welder had come for examination of a growth on his lip.

A Negro woman had come for treatment of sinusitis.

While ministering to the body, Clinic personnel also minister to the soul. In many cases there's little time to do an adequate counseling job, and for that reason a counselor is always on duty. But numerous times doctors, nurses and students have had opportunity to talk with patients about spiritual problems. Dr. Delbert Nelson of Chicago told of dealing with a man who had once been on the business staff at Harvard University. Nelson saw him a couple of times and talked to him about the sin that had dragged him to Skid Row. A man in his 40's, the patient made a profession of faith, and when Dr. Nelson last talked to him he was planning to return to his family.

Dr. John Elsen of Evanston, Illinois, who has been a sort of big brother to the Clinic personnel since the Clinic's inception, sums up the spiritual opportunities of this important phase of the Mission outreach: "We have had a number of men confess Christ in our Clinic, and there has been a great deal of spiritual growth on the part of many others. Probably the most notable thing that I have found over the years is the sense of companionship and willingness to listen on the part of both nurses and doctors in the Clinic. This is particularly true for men who have difficulty in maintaining their Christian testimony and have slipped off into drinking, etc., at times. This had been one of the most effective ministries in counseling and guiding these men on return. They many times feel more down and out than ever; and while we cannot condone their actions, we can show them that we are vitally concerned about them, even as Christ is."

Chapter 18

KEEPING THE LOWER LIGHTS BURNING

Go out quickly into the streets and lanes of the city, and bring in hither the poor, and the maimed, and the halt, and the blind (Luke 14:21*b*).

WHILE THE COMING of Harry Saulnier over a quarter of a century ago as keeper of the Old Lighthouse resulted in a much broader ministry sending the light to the four corners of the earth, Pacific Garden Mission must still be regarded basically as a Skid Row ministry. This was the original purpose, and it's still number one today despite the many facets of the work. However, some may actually wonder, for to the casual observer Skid Row seems to be vanishing along South State, especially with the addition of parking lots and the new Jones Commercial High School. But a walk along the street shows that it is much the same: the flophouses and honky-tonks are still there along with tattoo parlors, amusement palaces of "fun, art, and movies," theaters featuring nudist shows, and liquor stores where you can buy Five Star brandy at $1.25 a half pint, plus all sorts of other alcoholic beverages.

To complete the picture, pathetic figures still ply the sidewalk between dives, drowning their troubles in cheap wine and cursing the day they were born. But the light of the Mission still flashes through their dark, sin-swept world, calling them to hope, security, and a new life in Jesus Christ.

I talked with various veteran mission workers in direct contact with Skid Row men served by PGM. Some, I learned, are regulars who have been coming to the Old Lighthouse off and on for years. Yet the motto regarding these men is "Never give up on them." For there have been numerous cases of old-timers who finally trusted the Saviour after years of hearing the gospel and blossomed out in newness of life.

Among the old-timers they're praying for at PGM are such colorful characters as "Elmer Eder" who has been in and out of the Mission for more than 20 years. I saw him pass by the Mission door, a long green object in his hand. "He's an inventor," a worker explained. "He's invented a golf ball retriever and has been trying to get backers for it. First it was a rake made of Swedish steel. It looked good even to some of the fellows here, but Elmer insisted on managing the financial matters and that didn't work." A small, wiry man, Elmer, who professes to be saved, nonetheless can fight like a wildcat—except wildcats never hit with coke bottles and flowerpots, as Elmer has been known to do. Ask Joe Kurp, the two-ton night man, an ex-sparring partner of Jack Dempsey, who is glad he learned to duck in his fighting days.

"Bud Thompson," a Tennessean who wouldn't weigh 125 pounds soaking wet, according to Manfred Friedrich, has also been a periodic visitor for years. If he isn't in jail for drunkenness, he'll likely wind up at the Mission. One night in a fit of delirium tremens, he dreamed that he was in hell. Harry Saulnier was the chief. In his dream Thompson pleaded with Chief Saulnier for one more chance. Soon after, police carried him to the hospital to sew up an ugly gash he got in a fall. He got out immediately afterward and slept in an alley that night. Later he returned to the Mission, and each time he comes he is offered "one more chance."

Another old-timer that staff members pray for is "Phil Black," an artist, who "looks like a demon out of hell," as one man put it. His expression is constantly sarcastic, and he is a fighter when ruled by drink. Once he hit burly Manfred Friedrich six times. At one time it appeared Phil had made a stand for the Lord, and he worked in the Mission for a time, using his artistic ability to paint the Western mural on the walls of the Servicemen's Canteen. But soon he slipped back to the old life, falling into a worse state than ever.*

Thus, ministering to the flotsam of Skid Row brings its heartaches, but the happy stories on the other side of the ledger brighten the picture considerably. Day by day the Spirit of God is moving upon the hearts of men, and one by one they come to be made whole at the foot of the cross. In a typical year some 221,000 Skid Row men and women sign in and out of the Mission. Many of these, of course, are repeaters, but it is conservatively estimated the Mission annually proclaims the gospel to 200,000 drifters. In recent years, the harvests of souls among Skid Row people have been especially encouraging: 4368 in 1962, 4346 in 1963, and 3059 in 1964. The Mission has no way of knowing how many of those making professions actually "stick," but the percentage is high enough to keep the lower lights burning brightly.

The annual cost of maintaining the Skid Row ministry is considerable—186,000 dollars. (The total annual budget, including all phases of the PGM work, is 310,000 dollars.) Though the U.S. Government pours some 30 billion dollars each year into its new fight against poverty, the Mission receives no federal or local aid. Scores of churches include the Mission in their budgets, and certain other funds come in from Christian foundations and from legacies. But more than 85 percent of the funds are from individuals in the U.S., Canada, and elsewhere. A few, to be sure, send large gifts regularly, but such gifts are no more appreciated than the dollar or two dollars from a boy or girl, an elderly pensioner, or a shut-in. And scores of gifts come each month from all three groups.

"I am a boy 13 years old, but I am willing to give to Christ

---

*Though Elmer, Bud, and Phil are fictitious names, the men are real and the details true.

for the sake of other people," read one recent letter accompanied by a gift.

Letters from senior citizens often remind staff personnel of the widow whom Christ commended for giving her all: "I am sending a little gift for your wonderful work for the Lord. I am in my ninety-sixth year and am at the Covenant Home."

"I am old and have heart trouble and am not able to work. I get $57 per month Social Security, but I am sending you $5." "I am a widow. My income is $69.30 a month. Seven dollars isn't much but I want to help what I can."

Some of the gifts from the faithful seemingly stand little chance of getting through because of strangely worded addressing, but somehow Chicago postal employees manage to get this mail delivered. From Jamaica, West Indies, came a letter addressed in this fashion: "The City Garden Meschition, Chicago 5, Inonnia, U.S.A." A friend in Alaska, sending an anniversary gift, addressed his letter: "Pacific Guard and Mission, 87th Guard Anniversary, Chicago 5, Ill."

Some of those who write say they can't give but that they are praying. These letters are prized, along with the rest, for Harry Saulnier is constantly urging friends everywhere to pray regularly for the work "to turn back the powers of darkness that press in on us." In Arlington, Washington, four mothers meet every morning on schooldays and remember the Mission. Many shut-ins and elderly people, as well as the young and able-bodied, pray every day for the Old Lighthouse.

Even greater days lie ahead for the Mission, it would appear. With the completion of the section for families and homeless children, the Old Lighthouse will be at peak efficiency. But chances are Harry Saulnier won't let up. He hasn't said much about it, but another project has burdened his heart for years. "I've often wished we could have a farm where we could send the men who are saved, a place where we can work with them so that they will become established in the Lord," Harry told me. "But it's such a big undertaking. We're looking to God to find the place near Chicago and to tell us if and when we should add such a new division."

Keeping the Old Lighthouse in the Big City keeps all the keepers hopping. And it takes a lot of faith along the way.